The Vancouver Stock Exchange

The Vancouver Stock Exchange

Listing Rules, Policies and Procedures

Douglas R. Garrod

Elizabeth A. Watkins

Butterworths
Toronto and Vancouver

The Vancouver Stock Exchange: Listing Rules, Policies and Procedures
© 1990 Butterworths Canada Ltd.

Printed and bound in Canada.

The Butterworth Group of Companies

Canada:
Butterworths Canada Ltd.,
75 Clegg Road, MARKHAM, Ont. L3R 9Y6 and
409 Granville St., Ste 1455, VANCOUVER, B.C. V6C 1T2
Australia:
Butterworths Pty Ltd., SYDNEY, MELBOURNE, BRISBANE, ADELAIDE, PERTH, CANBERRA and HOBART
Ireland:
Butterworth (Ireland) Ltd., DUBLIN
Singapore:
Malayan Law Journal Ltd., SINGAPORE
New Zealand:
Butterworths of New Zealand Ltd., WELLINGTON and AUCKLAND
Puerto Rico:
Equity de Puerto Rico Inc., HATO REY
United Kingdom:
Butterworth & Co. (Publishers) Ltd., LONDON and EDINBURGH
United States:
Butterworth Legal Publishers, AUSTIN, Texas; BOSTON, Massachusetts; CLEARWATER, Florida (D & S Publishers); ORFORD, New Hampshire (Equity Publishing); ST. PAUL, Minnesota; and SEATTLE, Washington

Canadian Cataloguing in Publication Data

Garrod, Douglas R.
    The Vancouver Stock Exchange

ISBN 0-409-80949-7

1. Vancouver Stock Exchange. 2. Stock – exchange – Law and legislation – British Columbia.   I. Watkins, Elizabeth A.   II. Title.

KE274.5.V3G37   1989   332.64'2711   C90-091007-0

Sponsoring Editor: Janet Ames
Executive Editor: Eva Kossuth (Vancouver)
Editor: Susan Lagacé

To my mother and the memory of my father.

D.R.G.

To my parents.

E.A.W.

Preface

With the dramatic growth in the financial services industry in the past decade, there has been a concurrent dramatic growth in the need for acquiring knowledge about all aspects of corporate and personal financial matters. Moreover, as we approach 1990, there does not seem to be any lessening in this environment of growth. In fact, the issues are probably increasing in complexity which in turn adds to the need for greater knowledge.

"Going Public" by listing on a stock exchange and thereby raising equity funds from the general public has been one of those fields where the thirst for knowledge seems unquenchable. At the Vancouver Stock Exchange, we are very much aware of this need for knowledge and information.

How to list on the Vancouver Stock Exchange and raise equity financing through the facilities of the Exchange is one of those areas where a clear understanding of the procedures involved is essential to anyone associated with a company contemplating listing or already listed. Douglas Garrod and Elizabeth Watkins have provided an excellent source book covering all aspects of this process. Readers and users of this text will not only significantly widen their knowledge but also will no doubt enjoy the additional economic benefit of having their filings proceed more smoothly and therefore at greater speed and less cost.

Donald J. Hudson
President and Chief Executive Officer
Vancouver Stock Exchange

September 18, 1989

Acknowledgements

We would like to thank the Vancouver Stock Exchange for giving us confidential previews of many draft and final copies of numerous Listings Policy Statements and revisions to many Exchange Rules which changed during the writing of this book. We would also like to thank Donald J. Hudson, the President and Chief Executive Officer of the Exchange, for writing the Preface to this book.

Many thanks must also go to our respective secretaries, Lynn Robinson and Arlene McCulloch, for patiently typing and revising many drafts of the manuscript. As well, we would like to thank Lynn Robinson and the staff of the word processing centre at Campney & Murphy, who spent numerous hours retyping the manuscript and solving the many word processing problems associated with producing the final drafts of the manuscript.

We would also like to thank our respective partners at our law firms who gave us the encouragement and opportunity to write this book.

Table of Contents

Table of Contents

Abbreviations

Company Act   RSBC 1979, c.59, as amended.

Engineers Act   RSBC 1979, c.109, as amended.

Exchange   The Vancouver Stock Exchange.

Exchange Notice   A written notice of the Exchange disseminated to its Members, a copy of which is published in the Daily Bulletin.

Member   An individual, corporation or partnership holding at least one Seat on the Exchange.

Mortgage Brokers Act   RSBC 1979, c.283, as amended.

Registrar of Companies   The Registrar of Companies for British Columbia appointed under the *Public Service Act*, RSBC 1979, c.343, as amended.

Regulation to the
Securities Act   British Columbia Regulation 270/86, as amended.

SMF   Statement of Material Facts, being Form 24, prescribed pursuant to s.121 of the *Regulation to the Securities Act*.

Securities Act   SBC 1985, c.83, as amended.

Securities Commission   The British Columbia Securities Commission established under the *Securities Act*.

Special Committee	A committee formed in November, 1986 and comprised of the Superintendent of Brokers, the President and Vice-President, Listings of the Exchange, four Exchange Governors, one representative of an Exchange Member which reviewed and made recommendations on specific securities regulatory policies, the recommendations of which comprised the Special Committee Report.
Special Policy Committee	A committee formed in November, 1988 and comprised of the Superintendent of Brokers, the Chairman, President and Vice-President, Listings of the Exchange, the Managers of Policy & Planning and Filing & Listings of the Exchange, four Exchange Governors, one representative of an Exchange Member and one lawyer which reviewed and made recommendations on specific securities regulatory policies, the recommendations of which comprised the Special Policy Committee White Paper.
Superintendent of Brokers	The Superintendent of Brokers for British Columbia appointed under the *Public Service Act*, RSBC 1979, c.343, as amended.
Trust Company Act	RSBC 1979, c.412, as amended.

Table of Cases

Introduction

This book was written as an aid to professionals advising companies going public as well as those companies which already have their securities listed for trading on the Vancouver Stock Exchange. It is not a technical, procedural guide written exclusively for lawyers. While procedures and some technical matters are referred to out of necessity, the book concentrates on Exchange listings policy matters, since they form the Exchange's regulatory constraints on business decisions made by the management of listed companies and their professional advisers.

The book is organized by topic into 19 chapters. The first four chapters outline pre-listing and listing matters. Chapter 5 deals with the Exchange's prior approval requirements. Chapters 6, 7 and 8 cover the topic of financings by way of Exchange offerings, rights offerings and private placements. Chapters 9 to 13 discuss various Exchange policies relating to incentive stock options and shares for debt, two types of securities transactions Exchange-listed companies frequently undertake. Chapter 14 deals with the Exchange's regulations concerning principals' shares. Chapters 15 and 16 deal with amalgamations, acquisitions and the finder's fees which often accompany an acquisition. Chapter 17 discusses the Exchange's listing regulations respecting reactivations, the reorganization of what are, for the most part, inactive (or shell) companies. The last two chapters deal with the Exchange's timely disclosure rule and trading and delisting matters.

Between 1983 and 1987, the Vancouver Stock Exchange was reducing its listing regulations to writing, and developed and published over twenty new–some quite lengthy–listings policies; revised five new categories of Exchange Rules applicable only to listed companies; completely revised its listing application, Statement of Material Facts and Filing Statement forms, and developed two completely new listing procedures, the wrap-around application and the Initial Distribution System.

During 1988 and 1989, the number of listing regulation changes increased, due in large part to external pressures. The Exchange, recognizing that many of these listing regulations had become outdated or were inadequate, initiated and completed major revisions to these regulations. In October 1988, the Exchange announced several major listing regulation changes dealing with its timely disclosure policy, share purchase warrant policies, private placement and finder's fee rules. These represented the Exchange's response to the initiatives of the Ontario Securities Commission which had implemented a number of the recommendations in the Report of the Ontario Government's Thompson Committee.

In December of 1988, the Exchange announced that it had adopted several of the newly-created Special Policy Committee's recommendations and had increased its minimum listing requirements. These new requirements became effective on December 9, 1988 and imposed significantly higher listing requirements than those previously in force. For example, the minimum proceeds requirement associated with a non-resource company's initial public offering increased from $75,000.00 to $200,000.00. As part of the same initiative, in February of 1989, the Exchange announced completely new listing maintenance and reactivation requirements, as well as numerous revisions affecting reverse take-over regulations, rights offerings, Member sponsorship and delisting policies. At the same time, the Exchange announced that it would be revising the various categories of listed companies, and this latter revision, published on September 1, 1989, saw the creation of the Venture Company category and the Resource and Commercial/Industrial Company categories.

Since 1983, the number of listed companies and Exchange financing activity has expanded at a significant rate. As an example, in the 1982 calendar year, Exchange financings totalled $50.4 million; in 1985, that figure totalled $348 million; in 1987, $1.36 billion and, at the end of the 1988 calendar year, stood at $1.04 billion. On the listing side, the securities of 1,675 companies were listed for trading on the Exchange during the years 1983 to 1988 inclusive. Many of these new companies were and remain based outside of British Columbia.

This growth has led to a heightened demand for the expertise of professionals advising the management of companies going public, as well as listed companies. Lawyers, accountants and business consultants, to name a few, have had to quickly master the intricacies of a myriad of sometimes rapidly changing Exchange listing regulations.

No company has a right to have its securities listed for trading on the Exchange. Rather, it has only a legal privilege to do so. Moreover, the Exchange's jurisdiction over the business affairs of a company, once its securities are listed, is very wide. In this context (see Chapter 1), the Exchange has adopted a discretion which has been called the "fair, just and equitable" doctrine, which involves the Exchange making qualitative judgments about the business merits of the various transactions which come before it for review, and it underlies all of the listing regulations discussed in this book. Further, the "fair, just and equitable" doctrine is the basic premise for the Exchange's policies concerning acquisitions (see Chapter 18).

The Exchange has been criticized as being a minimum standards stock exchange. As noted in Chapters 3 and 5, the Exchange does have lower minimum listing requirements than do most other recognized stock exchanges in North America. It does this in the belief that legitimate junior resource and non-resource companies should be able to access the capital market, after having expended private investor funds on their business undertaking, in the same way that medium-size and large business enterprises have access to that market. The corollary to this, however, is that the Exchange tightly regulates these junior companies, relaxing its regulatory scrutiny as each company's business grows. This regulatory relaxation is evidenced in the Exchange prior-approval regulations, in which a listed company's ongoing Exchange filing requirements become less onerous the more developed its business becomes.

We note that, at this date, the acquisition policy of the Exchange (see Chapter 16) is being reviewed in the context of the Securities Commission's draft Local Policy Statement No. 3-07 (published on October 28, 1988). This review may result in a number of changes being made to the existing Exchange policy. Also under consideration at the time of writing is the role of promoters and a proposal permitting promoter's options to be granted by issuers as part of an initial distribution or Exchange offering. Announcements concerning these subjects probably will be made in the near future, and readers are cautioned to keep these revisions in mind once they are announced.

We have not discussed Exchange take-over bids, issuer bids or normal course issuer bids in this book. The Exchange has formalized the various Exchange Rule and Listings Policy Statement changes necessary to establish these and the regulations are similar in substance to the provisions of by-law No. 468 and the normal course issuer bid regulations of the Toronto Stock Exchange. The adoption of these new regulations permitted the Securities Commission to recognize the Exchange for the purposes of s.81(1)(a) of the *Securities Act*. Since books have been written on the subject of take-over bids, including Exchange bids, we have elected not to canvass these new regulations.

The book does not, in the main, deal with matters arising under the *Securities Act*, although reference is made to that statute when it is relevant to do so. Accordingly, readers are cautioned that whenever a listed company issues shares or other securities, whether on a private basis or to the public, resort must be made to the applicable *Securities Act* provisions.

As a final remark, we note that, in several instances, we refer to an unwritten policy of the Exchange. We use that phrase to indicate a practice or policy which the Exchange uses or enforces in the absence of a specific written rule dealing with the subject.

The Exchange makes available, free of charge to each listed company, a copy of its *Listings Policy and Procedures Manual* which contains a copy of each Exchange Listings Policy Statement referred to in this book. Other readers may purchase a copy of this *Manual* directly from the Exchange. Readers interested in obtaining copies of the Exchange Rules referred to in this book will have to purchase a copy of the Exchange's *By-Laws and Rules* book.

This book reflects Exchange Rules and Listings Policy Statements as they existed on September 30, 1989. All Listings Policy Statements referred to in the book are dated September 1, 1989.

Douglas R. Garrod
Elizabeth A. Watkins

September 30, 1989

CHAPTER ONE

The Vancouver Stock Exchange

GENERAL

During 1988, 3.5 billion shares representing a value of $3.3 billion were traded through the facilities of the Exchange. Of this $3.3 billion, $1.04 billion represented Exchange financings, $109.1 million represented initial distributions and $930.9 million represented other Exchange financings. In 1988, private placements accounted for $763.2 million. During 1987, 4.8 billion shares representing a value of $6.7 billion changed hands through the facilities of the Exchange. Of this $6.7 billion, $1.3 billion represented Exchange financings, $137.2 million represented initial distributions and $122.7 million represented other Exchange financings. $1.04 billion, or 83% of the total Exchange financings, represented private placements. The figures for these two years show that the Exchange is no longer a small regional stock exchange and has come a long way since April 26, 1907, the day the Exchange was incorporated by special act of the British Columbia Legislature. The Exchange subsequently opened for business in a small building located at 849 West Pender Street with twelve Member brokers. At December 31, 1988, with premises in the Stock Exchange Tower located at 609 Granville Street, the Exchange had 47 Member firms and the securities of 2,322 companies were listed for trading on its facilities.

The Exchange operates in a regulated environment. Pursuant to s.11 of the *Securities Act*, it is a recognized stock exchange for all purposes thereunder. In turn, the Exchange, particularly in the more recent past, has developed Rules and Listings Policy Statements which regulate the manner in which listed companies can undertake certain transactions. These Exchange Rules and Policy Statements are the subject of this book.

ORGANIZATION

The Exchange is headed by a Board of Governors of twenty-three individuals, at whose head is the Chairman. Of this total, fifteen represent industry Members (this includes the President of the Exchange), six are public governors and two are business governors. The Board of Governors meets quarterly. The Board of Governors, with two limited exceptions, does not become involved in specific applications made by listing applicants or listed companies to the Exchange. Rather, it approves, in the first instance, Rules and Listings Policy Statements. The application and enforcement of those Rules and Listings Policy Statements are left to Exchange staff. Any subsequent changes to the provisions of either type of listing regulation must be approved by the Board. The two areas where the Board of Governors directly reviews a listing matter are under Exchange Rules F.2.25.1 and 25.2 which require prior Exchange approval to be obtained by an individual who is an employee of a brokerage firm, excluding its directors, officers and partners, and who proposes to become a director of a listed company (see Chapter 2). The other area where the Board of Governors reviews specific listing matters involves the area where, under Exchange Rules F.2.26 and 2.27, an employee of a brokerage firm, excluding its directors, officers and partners, proposes to enter certain transactions with a listed company (see Chapter 12).

One of the more important Board committees is the Market Functions Committee. This Committee is currently comprised of nine industry representatives, including two Governors, the President of the Exchange and the Exchange's Vice-President, Listings. The Committee meets on a monthly basis, with one or more of the Securities Commission's staff in attendance, to initiate and review listings policies and procedures and to adopt recommendations for consideration by the Exchange's Executive Committee. This Committee, made up of the Exchange Chairman, Vice-Chairman, Secretary/Treasurer, Past Chairman and President, plus three other Exchange Governors, must then approve these recommendations for transmittal to the Board of Governors for its consideration. The Market Functions Committee, from time to time, also gives policy direction to the Exchange's Listing Committee which is the most significant Committee as far as listed companies are concerned, since it is this Committee, comprised solely of Exchange staff members, which renders individual decisions on each application presented to it for its consideration.

Another significant Board committee is the Pre-Listing Review Committee which reviews all companies proposing to list on the Exchange and all companies proposing a reverse take-over (see Chapter 3).

LISTINGS DEPARTMENT

Most dealings of a listed company will be with one or more members of the Listings Department. Routine filings such as corporate name changes, private placements, incentive stock options, shares for debt and transfers within escrow are handled by assistants to listings officers. If these filings raise new or controversial issues, then these assistants may turn to a listings officer or senior listings officer for direction and advice. Reorganizations, reverse take-overs, and acquisitions are, in the main, handled in the Listings Department by listings officers and senior listings officers. These individuals also generally review material changes disclosed in Filing Statements as well as Exchange offerings qualified by SMFs.

The regulatory approach taken by the Exchange is more than that countenanced by the doctrine of full, true and plain disclosure. Rather, the Exchange historically has adopted what is often called a blue sky approach. That is, it exercises its discretion in a manner which closely typifies the "fair, just and equitable" doctrine. In this respect, the Exchange makes qualitative judgments about the business merits of the various transactions which are put before it for its review. This jurisdiction was discussed by the Corporate and Financial Services Commission in the case of *In the Matter of Syn-Trac Industries Ltd.* (October 31, 1977). While in that case the express issue was the jurisdiction of the Superintendent of Brokers to reject an SMF, it was noted by the Corporate and Financial Services Commission that the Exchange had for some time exercised a blue-sky approach when vetting SMFs. That is, the Exchange looked to matters beyond disclosure issues, matters which were concerned with the business merits of a proposed transaction.

The Listings Department is headed by the Vice-President, Listings, who, in turn, reports to the Exchange's Executive Vice-President. Reporting to him are two managers, namely, the Manager, Listings and Filings and the Manager, Policy and Planning. The Vice-President is in charge overall; the Manager, Listings and Filings is responsible for the supervision of the day-to-day work flow and decisions made by senior listings officers and listings officers while the Manager, Policy and Planning, is primarily responsible for the development of securities regulatory policy and planning matters.

Listed companies will deal most often with the Exchange Listings Committee. The Committee is comprised of the Vice-President, Listings, who acts as its Chairman, the two Managers and the Department's senior listings officers. This Committee, which meets on a weekly basis, is somewhat unique amongst the recognized Canadian stock exchanges because, with the two limited exceptions noted above which are within the exclusive jurisdiction of the Exchange Governors, it makes the final decision on behalf of the Exchange regarding all listings matters. While the Committee receives and reviews written submissions, it does not sit publicly nor hear evidence in the manner of most regulatory tribunals. The Committee does not permit a representative of a listed company to come before it to make verbal representations, and it communicates its decisions on specific matters through the listings officer with specific conduct of the

3

listed company's file. While the President of the Exchange has the authority to overturn a decision of the Listings Committee, he very rarely exercises this authority. There may be drawbacks to this procedure, but the fact the Exchange Membership does not have any input into the day-to-day listing decisions which are made by the Listings Committee is viewed as beneficial since there is no danger that the public will perceive the public interest being affected by the interests of the various Member firms. The one exception to this procedure relates to the Pre-Listing Review Committee.

It should be pointed out that the Listings Committee may rehear a particular application and, if it is so inclined, may reverse an earlier ruling so long as there are new facts or fresh arguments presented. In most cases, the listed company will change the structure of its proposed transaction to comply more fully with the wishes of the Listings Committee and, as well, there is usually, but not always, a facilitating movement made in the previous posture of the Listings Committee.

APPEALS FROM EXCHANGE DECISIONS

Under s.15 of the *Securities Act*, a person directly affected by a direction, decision, order or ruling of the Exchange may appeal by applying for a hearing and review of the matter under Part 17 of the *Act*. These appeals, which do not usually proceed by way of a *de novo* hearing, were previously heard by the Corporate and Financial Services Commission; now, under the Act, they are heard by the Securities Commission.

Over recent years only a few cases involving listings decisions have been appealed. In a relatively early case, *In the Matter of Bali Exploration Ltd.*, Corporate and Financial Services Commission (July 27, 1976), the Exchange refused to accept a Filing Statement disclosing the issuance of certain debentures by the listed company because it was not satisfied that the listed company had the ability to repay the debentures. It was argued on appeal that the Exchange had no power to usurp the business judgment of the listed company's directors. In response, the Commission stated that a company objecting to the decision of the Exchange must point to something more than a mere difference of opinion between corporate management and the Exchange. The company must be able to show that the Exchange acted oppressively, or in bad faith, or in some other fashion abused its power.

Those principles were reaffirmed by the Corporate and Financial Services Commission case *In the Matter of James Industries Inc.*, (May 4, 1979); *In the Matter of Major Resources Ltd.*, (June 29, 1979); and *In the Matter of Mariah Resources Ltd.*, (December 21, 1984), where the Commission was of the view that in deciding on the acceptance or refusal of a listing, the decision of the Exchange as to what is or is not in the public interest is one with which the Commission will not interfere unless it felt the decision was wrong.

In an Exchange appeal heard by the Securities Commission, the same non-interventionist role was re-affirmed: see *In the Matter of Argonaut Resources Ltd.*, (November 5, 1987). Accordingly, the merits of an Exchange decision, as a result of these decisions, are extremely difficult to attack on appeal to the Securities Commission. However, the Securities Commission will hold a *de novo* hearing, and substitute its own decision for that of the Exchange's when it concludes that, based on principles of natural justice, the Exchange has not acted fairly in a procedural sense. In *In the Matter of Murex Clinical Technologies Corporation*, Securities Commission, (March 23, 1989), the Exchange had considered a particular escrow release application and had made a ruling on this application. The Commission concluded that, because of what it considered to be significant procedural defects, it should consider the application itself by holding a *de novo* hearing. At this writing, an appeal from the decision of the Securities Commission had been filed in the British Columbia Court of Appeal by the Exchange.

CHAPTER TWO

Pre-Listing Matters

GENERAL

Many of the Exchange's listing requirements, and many of the Superintendent of Brokers' going public rules, are retroactive in nature: they apply to transactions which have been entered into at a time when a company is in its private, pre-public stage and when the company is not under the direct jurisdiction of the Superintendent. This is true in the case of companies incorporated under the *Company Act*, federally or extra-provincially, because the Exchange's regulations, and the *Securities Act*, do not create any significant differences between provincial and extra-provincial issuers. In the latter case, the provisions of Listings Policy Statement No. 13 prohibit a listing of a company's shares which has not complied with all British Columbia securities regulatory policies in the year prior to the date of the listing application. A British Columbia securities regulatory policy includes a requirement arising under the *Securities Act*, a Local Policy Statement or Notice issued by the Securities Commission, a By-law or Rule of the Exchange and an Exchange Listings Policy Statement. Not only will the Exchange not list the shares of a company which has not complied with British Columbia securities regulatory policies, but the Superintendent will not accept a prospectus for filing under the *Securities Act* if these rules and regulations are not adhered to. So pervasive are these rules that they apply to even the first issuances of shares which a company undertakes. Therefore it is important that these rules be understood and fully complied with.

CORPORATE MATTERS

A. Company Name

Under the practice guidelines set forth under the *Company Act*, a name should have a distinctive element followed by a descriptive element. By virtue of s.16 of the *Act*, a company, other than a specially limited company, must have as the last word of its corporate name Limited, Incorporated or Corporation or the abbreviation Ltd., Inc. or Corp. A specially limited company must have one of the foregoing words or abbreviations followed by the bracketed words (Non-Personal Liability) or the letters (N.P.L.). For all purposes, the words Limited or Incorporated or Corporation or Non-Personal Liability are interchangeable with their abbreviations Ltd., Inc., Corp. or N.P.L. Only one of the words Limited, Incorporated or Corporation or its abbreviation may be used.

Under ss. 17 and 18 of the *Act*, where a company or an extra-provincial company has, for any reason, a name identical with that of another corporation which has previously been incorporated or registered in British Columbia, or a name so nearly resembling that name that, in the opinion of the Registrar of Companies, it is likely to confuse or mislead, the Registrar may in writing, giving his reasons, order the company to change its name to one acceptable to the Registrar.

The test in respect of similar names under Exchange policy is whether the names would confuse an average reasonable investor of intelligence acting with ordinary caution as opposed to an unwary, incautious or hurried securities buyer; see *In the Matter of Equinox Resources Ltd.*, Securities Commission (June 22, 1987). The Exchange Listings Department has a name reservation service which should be used by companies making an application for an initial listing or proposing to effect a change in their corporate name after being listed.

B. Directors and Officers

Under the provisions of s.132 of the *Act*, a reporting, and therefore listed, company must have a minimum of three directors. Under s.133 of the same statute, a majority of the company's directors must be Canadian residents and at least one director must be a resident of British Columbia. The definition of director in s.1(1) of the Act includes an individual who, while not a named director, is actually performing the acts of a director. Such a person would be liable for his acts as a director in the same way that named, and properly elected, directors are liable.

Every director of a listed company, in exercising his powers and performing his functions, is required by s.142(1) of the *Act* to act honestly, in good faith and in the best interests of the company at all times. Under the same subsection, a director must also exercise the care, diligence and skill of a reasonably prudent person. As set forth in s.141(1) of the *Act*, the role of directors as a whole is to manage, or supervise the management of, the affairs and business of the company.

Under the provisions of s.138(1) of the *Act*, while there are no qualifications specified for directors, a number of disqualifications are set out. In addition to age and mental incompetency disqualifications, one cannot be a director of a listed company if a person is an undischarged bankrupt, has been convicted of an offence in connection with the promotion, formation or management of a company, or one involving fraud, unless five years have elapsed since sentencing or unless the British Columbia Supreme Court orders otherwise. Furthermore, a person will be disqualified if that person's registration in any capacity under the *Securities Act* or the *Mortgage Brokers Act* has been cancelled, unless the Superintendent of Brokers orders otherwise or unless five years have elapsed since the cancellation.

The provisions of Exchange Rule F.2.25 prohibit any employees of a brokerage firm from being a director of a listed company without the prior approval of the Exchange, whether the employee is a British Columbia resident or whether the firm falls under the jurisdiction of the Exchange, unless the employee is a director, officer, or partner of or in a brokerage firm. These applications are considered by the Exchange's Board of Governors. Exchange approval, as a matter of Exchange practice, is never given. It should be noted that the Rule extends beyond what would otherwise be thought of as the jurisdictional boundaries of the Exchange, since it applies to employees of brokerage firms not under the Membership jurisdiction of the Exchange.

Under the provisions of Exchange Rule B.1.11.1, a listed company must be managed by individuals who have expertise in the area of the company's actual or proposed undertaking. If the company does not have such management, then it must retain a consultant who does.

A special committee of the directors, called the audit committee, is the only mandatory directors' committee required by the *Company Act*. This requirement is set out in s.211(1) of the *Act*. The audit committee must be comprised of at least three directors, a majority of whom cannot also be officers of the listed company. The purpose of the committee is to review with the company's auditor every audited financial statement of the listed company, and to report to the full board of directors, prior to the financial statements being presented to the company's shareholders.

With respect to officers, each company formed under the *Act* must, by virtue of s.157(1), have a president, who must also be a director of the company, and a secretary. For the purposes of a listed company, these two offices must be held by two separate individuals. The disqualifications set out in the same *Act* which apply to directors also apply to officers. Each officer must, in exercising his powers and performing his duties, exercise these powers and perform these duties to the same exacting standards required of a director. Because of the effect of the interaction between the audit committee requirements and the rules concerning the president and secretary, a listed company with only three directors will have to appoint a secretary who is not a director.

C. Auditor

Under the provisions of s.202(1) of the *Act,* each listed company must have an auditor. Auditors are elected, or re-elected, at the company's annual general meeting. An auditor of a listed company, with few exceptions, must be a person who is a member, or a partnership whose partners are members, in good standing with the Canadian Institute of Chartered Accountants or the Certified General Accountants Association of British Columbia. The auditor must be independent of the company, its affiliates and its directors and officers.

The role of the auditor is to audit the annual financial statements of the company. He must submit his audit report to the members of the company's audit committee prior to the report being considered by the company's directors. His report must, after being approved by the company's directors, be presented to the company's shareholders.

D. Registrar and Transfer Agent

Under the provisions of ss. 65, 66 and 67 of the *Act,* each company must maintain a register of its current registered shareholders and a record of each allotment (or issuance) and transfer in the registered ownership of its shares. Because of the complexity involved in keeping these three sets of records for a publicly traded company, companies are authorized to appoint, respectively, a registrar and a transfer agent to perform these two related functions. Instead of the company itself keeping these records, s.69(1) of the *Act* permits a company to retain a trust company registered under the *Trust Company Act* to perform these services. Exchange Rule B.1.11.3 requires a listed company to have a registrar and transfer agent with an office in the City of Vancouver.

E. Independent Consultant

A company filing a prospectus with the Superintendent of Brokers or an SMF with the Superintendent and the Exchange, will, by virtue of the Securities Commission Local Policy Statements Nos. 3-01 and 3-04 (February 1, 1987), be required to file with that prospectus or SMF a report describing, in some detail, the particular assets of the company on which the proceeds of the company's public offering are to be expended. This rule also applies to situations where a listed company acquires a material asset. The company will be required to retain the services of an independent consultant prior to going public.

Technical reports on natural resource properties located in Canada must, in accordance with the provisions of Securities Commission Local Policy Statement No. 3-01 (February 1, 1987):

- in the case of a report on a mining property, be prepared by an independent mining engineer or geologist who is a member in good standing of the Association of Professional Engineers, or by a geologist who is a Fellow in the Geological Association of Canada, or by other qualified persons acceptable to the Superintendent; or
- in the case of a report on an oil and gas property, be prepared by an independent petroleum engineer who is a member in good standing of an appropriate Association of Professional Engineers, or by another qualified person acceptable to the Superintendent.

Where a property is located within British Columbia, the *Engineers Act* requires the practice of engineering be performed by a Professional Engineer registered with the Association of Professional Engineers of British Columbia as a resident member or licenced to practice in British Columbia as a non-resident licensee. In the case of an out-of-province or out-of-country property, the author must be a member of a similar acceptable professional association.

Where an oil and gas property is located in the United States of America, membership in the Society of Petroleum Engineers of the American Institute of Mining and, or, membership in the American Institute of Professional Geologists is preferable for an author who is a U.S. resident, as is registration in the appropriate engineering association of the state in which the property is located.

A technical report respecting a non-resource asset must be prepared by a suitably qualified person in accordance with the provisions of Securities Commission Local Policy Statement No. 3-04 (February 1, 1987). The author must be capable of assessing the technical and operational aspects involved, of assessing and evaluating the marketing aspects, of forming an opinion on the reasonableness of cost estimates and of appraising the value of the assets which are the subject of funding. The following are suggested qualification guidelines for authors:

- ten years related academic/industrial experience;
- two to four years specific and relevant experience; and
- experience with consulting assignments of the type involved.

Where one individual does not possess sufficient expertise to deal with all aspects of a technical report, a joint report compiled by more than one individual possessing in aggregate the required expertise will be accepted.

Except for the situation described below, the author or joint authors of a report (this rule also applies to a resource property report) should have no direct, indirect or contingent interest in the securities of the company, in the property or program which is the subject of a report nor have any form of association with the vendor of such property. Where persons associated with the company possess the qualifications indicated above, a technical report may be prepared by them, provided their report is accompanied by a letter from an independent qualified consultant commenting on the adequacy and credibility of the contents of the company's report.

F. Share Certificates

Share certificates representing the common shares (as well as any other listed security) of listed companies are subject to very strict requirements, by virtue of Listings Policy Statement No. 14. These have been designed to ensure there are adequate safeguards and protection against forgery. Since these certificates will be required once the company becomes listed, it is important to ensure, towards the latter part of the private stage, that the certificates which are going to be used are not only acceptable but are also available in sufficient quantities for use by the company's registrar and transfer agent. The important minimum requirements are as follows:

1. *General*

- certificates must conform with the requirements of the corporate legislation under which the company is incorporated;
- certificates must be printed in a manner acceptable to the Exchange by a bank note company, its affiliate or other security printer recognized for this purpose by the Exchange;
- models, proofs and/or specimens of all certificates must be submitted to the Exchange prior to being circulated. The recognized bank note companies are familiar with Exchange requirements and procedures and, upon instructions from the company, will generally submit models, proofs and specimens of certificates for review by the Exchange;
- changes in the form or design of certificates must not be made without the prior consent of the Exchange.

2. *Paper*

- all paper used for certificates must be of an excellent grade of security bond paper of adequate weight and strength;
- all certificates must be 12" by 8" (30.8 cm by 20.32 cm) and must contain multi-colored, randomly scattered planchettes throughout the paper.

3. *Steel Engraving (Intaglio) Content*

• the face of the certificates must contain printing by at least one intaglio plate printing process. The intaglio printing process must carry a geometric lathe design and must be in a distinctive colour other than black.

4. *Transfer and Registration*

• all certificates must provide for transfer and registration in the City of Vancouver and the name of the registrar and transfer agent and registrar must be stated on the face of the certificate. When certificates are also transferable in other cities, reference to this must be indicated on the face of the certificate.

5. *Back*

• the back of a certificate, containing a form of assignment, may be surface printed (lithographed) but must be printed in a colour other than black (preferably in brown).

6. *Other*

• trade marks, trade names or logos may be used on the face of the certificate however they may not replace the proper corporate name which must be printed prominently and in black on the certificate;
• the general or promissory text must be printed in black;
• no impression may be made on the face of the certificate by means of a hand stamp except to inscribe a date and the name of the registered holder;
• the CUSIP number must appear on the upper right quadrant of the certificate.

7. *Exempt Companies*

In addition to the above requirements, the intaglio printing content for certificates of exempt companies must include the following:

• the denomination panel must contain intaglio printing in an underlying tint of the colour used in the panel(s) or border;
• the general or promissory text must be printed using the intaglio process in script style lettering;
• the face portion of the certificate must include a fine line engraving in black as a vignette. The vignette design should include some plainly discernible features of at least a part of the human form and should contain a wide range of tones.

Certificates containing any additional security features, such as latent images or micro-lettering, will be acceptable provided the minimum requirements set out above are met.

G. CUSIP Number

CUSIP is an abbreviation for the Committee on Uniform Security Identification Procedures. The provisions of Listings Policy Statement No. 14 require all certificates representing listed securities to have a CUSIP number. This security identification number, issued by Standard & Poor's Corporation in New York, is transmitted in Canada by Standard & Poor's Corporation and the Exchange. A CUSIP number for an Exchange-listed security may be obtained through either agency. These numbers, which may take several weeks to obtain, should be applied for well in advance of the time securities regulatory acceptance of filing documents is anticipated. It should be noted that a new, supplemental number is required for share purchase warrants and share purchase rights which are to be called for trading. A completely new CUSIP number is generally required whenever a company changes its name.

PRE-PUBLIC SHARE TRANSACTIONS

A. General

The first stage in the going public process is typically called the private stage because it is a period during which there can be no public trading of any of the company's securities. Specifically, and by virtue of s.42 of the *Securities Act*, a company cannot issue its shares to the public generally; those who buy shares in this stage must do so under some very restrictive *Act* exemptions, and these investors may not resell their shares to the public generally until the company's shares become listed for trading on the Exchange.

There are, from a securities regulatory point of view, three types of shares: seed capital shares and principals' shares are sold for cash; property shares are issued as consideration, either in whole or in part, for assets acquired by the company. There are also some special rules of the Securities Commission and the Exchange for each category of shares: failure to comply with these rules can have serious adverse consequences for the company and its shareholders. For example, additional consideration may have to be paid for certain shares.

B. Seed Capital Shares

Shares sold for cash during the private stage to private investors are called seed capital shares because they are issued to raise the initial, or seed, capital of the company. These types of shares, by virtue of Securities Commission Local Policy Statement No. 3-08 (February 1, 1987) and Exchange Rule B.1.13.2, must be sold at a price per share equal to or greater than $0.25. Furthermore, the applicable rules require that at least $150,000.00 be raised by resource companies, and $275,000.00 in the case of industrial companies, by issuing seed capital shares (see Exchange Rule B.1.13.3). Practically speaking, this means that a private company issuing shares at the minimum price of $0.25 per share must have issued at least 600,000 of its common shares in the case of a resource company and 1,100,000 shares in the case of a non-resource company prior to the filing of its prospectus with the Superintendent of Brokers.

Depending on the number of and price paid for seed capital shares, they may have to be held (or pooled as it is called) by the private investors after the company becomes listed on the Exchange pursuant to the provisions of what is called a pooling agreement, the form of which has been prescribed by the Superintendent in an Appendix to Local Policy Statement No. 3-08. Under this Local Policy Statement, only shares sold at a price less than 50% of the company's first public offering price must be pooled and only if more than 10,000 shares have been acquired by the private investor. If the shares are required to be pooled, 25% of the total amount pooled will be released from the pooling restriction on the day of listing; the remaining 75% are released in equal amounts each of the following three months until all are released at the end of nine months from the original listing on the Exchange. In the event a listing on the Exchange has not been obtained within twelve months of the date of the company's prospectus qualifying its first public offering, then all the pooled shares will be released automatically.

There may be instances where the Superintendent of Brokers will restrict or otherwise agree to vary the terms of release, particularly in the case of a company engaged in research and development. These situations are dealt with on a case-by-case basis.

The share certificates representing the pooled shares must be held by an acceptable trustee or pooling manager, usually the trust company which has become the company's registrar and transfer agent, and the shares cannot be transferred while they remain pooled without the written consent of the Superintendent of Brokers (if the company is not listed) or the Exchange (if the company is, at the time of the transfer application, listed on the Exchange). It should be noted that if shares are required to be pooled, a pooling agreement must be signed by each private investor, as well as the trustee or pooling manager, and a copy of that agreement must be filed by the company with both the Superintendent and the Exchange.

Special rules and restrictions apply to any seed capital shares purchased by brokerage firms, stockbrokers, other employees of brokerage firms and their associates. These rules are set forth in Securities Commission Local Policy Statement No. 3-30 (February 1, 1987) and provide that the maximum number of shares held by all persons in this group is the lesser of 150,000 shares or 10% of the issued shares outstanding after the first public offering. No one of these persons (other than a brokerage firm itself) may hold more than the lesser of 50,000 shares or 5% of the issued shares outstanding after the first public offering. No shares held by any person in this group, irrespective of the price paid for their shares, may be sold prior to the expiry of six months from listing of the company's shares on the Exchange and, thereafter, where more than 10,000 shares have been acquired, 25% of the shares will be released on expiry of this six month hold period and 25,000 shares after each subsequent three month period, provided seven days notice of the intended sale is filed with the Superintendent of Brokers and the Exchange.

The Special Policy Committee has made several recommendations affecting these rules. A maximum of 300,000 shares may be sold to the persons mentioned above as a group. No one of these persons (other than a brokerage firm which may acquire up to 150,000 shares) may own more than 50,000 shares. Persons included in the above-mentioned group must hold, irrespective of the price paid for their shares, all their seed capital shares for a minimum period of six months after the listing of the company's shares on the Exchange. Fifty percent of all these pooled shares will be released after the expiry of this six month period. The balance of fifty percent are released in two equal share blocks at the end of each three month period following the expiry of the initial six month hold period.

C. Performance Shares

In 1983, with the growth in non-resource companies going public and subsequently applying for a listing on the Exchange, the Superintendent of Brokers revised the then-existing escrow share rules to permit the issuance of two quite different types of escrow shares. Securities Commission Local Policy Statement No. 3-07 (February 6, 1987) deals with these two types of escrow shares. The first type, called principals' shares, may only be issued to the principals of a particular company, for a minimum cash price of $0.01 per share. A maximum of 750,000 such shares may be issued, irrespective of the existing and proposed capitalization of the company. A second type of escrow share, commonly called earn-out shares, may be issued as consideration for a property or asset having what is called a determinate value. These types of shares, the subject of very complex rules, are mainly issued by non-resource companies. Up to the lesser amount of 60% of the outstanding shares of the company (after its initial distribution) or 3,000,000 shares may be issued. The Securities Commission intends to revise Local Policy Statement, No. 3-07 and published a draft Local Policy Statement No. 3-07 on October 28, 1988. The rules set out in this draft Policy Statement form the subject of most of the balance of this Chapter.

The substantive portion of draft Local Policy Statement No. 3-07 sets forth four general rules. It provides that no share or other consideration may be issued or paid for what is called an excess asset. This means an asset, including an interest in another company, or property which is not related to the current business or undertaking of the company. Where any performance shares are issued by the company going public to a wholly-owned holding company owned by an individual who is a principal, then the appropriate written undertaking must be given to the Superintendent of Brokers not to change the share ownership of the holding company in the absence of the approval of the Superintendent (if the company's securities are unlisted) or the Exchange (if the securities of the company are listed on the Exchange). Where a company contemplates, either as full or partial consideration for the acquisition of an asset or property, the issuance of shares, the agreement covering the acquisition must be drawn up subject to regulatory approval. The fourth, and last, general rule requires a minimum issuance price, deemed or otherwise, of $0.01 per performance share.

Parts 4 and 5 of draft Local Policy Statement No. 3-07 deal with what are called trading shares; shares which are not subject to any performance restrictions. These shares are commonly referred to as free-trading shares.

In the case of non-resource companies, that number of trading shares, issuable at a minimum price of $0.25 as fixed by Securities Commission Local Policy Statement No. 3-08 (February 1, 1987), (a significant departure from the previous rule which required a minimum issue price equal to the initial public offering price) must be at least equal in value to the aggregate of (a) the amount of cash paid in as share capital, (b) the fair market value, supported by a current valuation opinion, of any non-cash assets, and (c) the company's retained earnings less its accumulated deficit. Where the company has an accumulated deficit and where it has incurred expenses directly related to its undertaking and these expenses have contributed to its accumulated deficit, additional trading shares may be issued up to the aggregate of the amounts specified in (a) and (b) above if the expenses have contributed or are likely to positively contribute to the company's future operations. It is recognized that a company may carry on its undertaking through a subsidiary, and where there is no current valuation opinion respecting the company's investment in that subsidiary, then the rules

17

noted above must be followed to determine the number of trading shares that may be issued by the company for acquiring its interest in the subsidiary. It should be noted that the Superintendent of Brokers may exclude any amount from these calculations which is not considered appropriate or where the number of trading shares to be issued is, in the opinion of the Superintendent, unconscionable.

In the case of resource companies, and in the case of unproven properties, a distinction is made between arm's length and non-arm's length transactions. This is not the case with the non-resource trading share rules. There are three applicable rules in the non-arm's length area which are set out in draft Local Policy Statement No. 3-07. No shares may be issued for properties of unproven value irrespective of the number of properties acquired. While cash may be paid, the amount is restricted to the vendor's out-of-pocket expenses. Where a property can be said to have substantial merit, additional consideration in the form of either shares or a reasonable net profits interest may be paid; this represents an exception to the first rule. As a general rule, a 15% net profits interest, based on the acquisition of a 100% interest in a particular property being acquired, will be considered reasonable. Non-arm's length in these circumstances is defined to include, in general, a transaction between the company and any principal, insider, promoter, associate or affiliate of the company. The term principal for these purposes, and for the purposes of eligible recipients of performance shares, is defined to mean a director or promoter of the company, a full time key employee of the company or an operating subsidiary which the company controls, a person who has provided key services or contributed a fundamental asset to the company, and any wholly- owned holding company of any of these individuals.

The vending rules regulating arm's length acquisitions of unproven properties remain much the same in the draft Local Policy Statement as Local Policy Statement No. 3-07 (February 6, 1987). Resource properties of unproven value must be acquired on an option basis, and must be paid for by not less than four option payments in blocks of shares not exceeding 50,000 in number, one block of which may be issued before the securities of the company become listed on the Exchange. The remaining blocks, issuable in a minimum of three blocks or stages, may be issued only after acceptable engineering reports recommending further work on the property in question have been filed. Up-front cash consideration may be paid, generally, only to reimburse the vendor for out-of-pocket costs, and cash instalments may be paid to maintain property rights. Additional consideration may be paid where a property can be regarded as having substantial merit. This consideration may be in the form of a reasonable production or profits interest which are suggested by the draft Local Policy Statement to be not more than a 5% net smelter interest or a 20% net profits interest. As well, additional share compensation may be paid in excess of the 200,000 share limit if the property commences commercial production.

Trading shares also may be issued by a resource company for acquiring a resource property of proven value equal to, or less than, the number of the quotient of the proven value divided by $0.25. It should be noted that the pooling rules discussed immediately above under the heading Seed Capital Shares apply to all trading shares issued for other than a cash consideration.

Parts 6 to 9, inclusive, of Securities Commission draft Local Policy Statement No. 3-07 (October 28, 1988) deal with what are called performance shares. This is the new name given to what are now called earn-out shares. The significant difference between the present policies and the proposed policies is that the proposed policies require that performance shares be issued for cash; no longer will there be the need for what is often a contrived vend-in transaction to generate a substantial control position for a company's principals.

Part 6 of draft Local Policy Statement No. 3-07 sets out two fundamental rules. Resource companies, companies engaged in mining, gas, oil or exploration work, may issue only up to 750,000 performance shares to their principals. All other types of companies may issue performance shares to their principals providing that the performance share percentage, in relation to the total number of issued and outstanding voting shares after the completion of the company's initial public offering, does not exceed 65%. It must be pointed out that non-resource companies will no longer be permitted to issue the equivalent of 750,000 principals' shares in addition to issuing the equivalent of earn- out shares. However, it should be noticeable immediately that the current 3,000,000 share limit is proposed to be abolished for non-resource companies. Conversely, the current 750,000 share maximum is proposed to be retained for resource companies.

After the expiry of a phase-in period, performance shares, under the regime set out in Part 7 of the October 28, 1988 draft Local Policy Statement, must be a separate class of a listed company's securities, having the following attributes:

- one vote attached to each share;
- convertible on a 1:1 basis at the option of the holder into trading shares on terms noted below;
- non-participating in any way until conversion into trading shares;
- be cancelled by the company within 10 years from the later of their issuance and the effective date of the company's prospectus qualifying its initial public offering;
- be non-transferable except to the estate of a deceased or to those entitled to acquire them in the event of a holders bankruptcy, other principals or incoming principals, or the company itself.

A significant right granted under the proposed Policy Statement enables a shareholder or shareholders owning more than 5% of the outstanding voting shares of the company to convene a general meeting of shareholders for the purpose of considering a resolution to cancel all or a part of the outstanding performance shares. The draft Policy requires, as a precondition for such a meeting, that the company be essentially dormant for a period of 12 consecutive months. At such a meeting, the holders of performance shares are precluded from voting *any* voting shares of the company which they may own.

Other provisions dealing with the exchange of performance shares, adjustments to the conversion formula, and reclassification provisions in the event of consolidations, mergers or amalgamations are dealt with in the balance of Part 7.

Part 8 of the draft Policy Statement deals with the manner in which performance shares may be converted into trading shares, that is, common voting shares of the company. In general, there are two rules dealing with general prohibitions respecting the conversion of performance shares of both a resource company and an industrial, or non-resource, company. The operation of the general prohibition precludes conversion when the company is insolvent, is not in good standing with all stock exchanges and securities commissions having jurisdiction over it, or with the Registrar of Companies (or similar authority), and when the company is a dormant issuer within the meaning of that term as defined in Securities Commission Local Policy Statement No. 3-35 (October 13, 1989). The second basic prohibition is that the actual conversion into trading shares may occur only once in any given 12 month period.

The proposed conversion rules for natural resource companies, as prescribed by the draft Local Policy Statement No. 3-07, with two minor exceptions, are identical to the escrow share release of the Exchange rules discussed in Chapter 14. The first exception relates to the fact that where the listed company's administrative expenses exceed 33% of exploration and development expenditures, then only one-half of the number of shares which otherwise may be converted are allowed to be converted. Under the Exchange's Listings Policy Statement No. 18, the Exchange exercises its discretion, on occasion, to prohibit any release. Furthermore, in such circumstances, only a maximum of 25% of the original number of performance shares may be converted in any one year. This, as well, is discretionary in the Exchange's Policy Statement.

In the case of non-resource companies, the number of performance shares which may be converted in any 12 month period will be determined by dividing the cumulative cash flow not already used in a calculation under the formula by the earn-out price. The term earn-out price is defined as being the product of the initial offering price multiplied by the earn-out factor, the latter being defined as the number obtained by squaring the performance share percentage, expressed as a decimal, and multiplying that number by four.

After performance shares become eligible for conversion, 14 days written notice must be given to the Superintendent of Brokers, the Exchange and, if the notice is given by a performance shareholder, to the company. Amongst other documents, a calculation prepared by the company's auditor of the number of shares to be converted must be provided to the parties named above. If neither the Superintendent nor the Exchange object to the conversion within the 14 days, the conversion may proceed.

Transfers of performance shares are covered by Part 9 of the draft Local Policy Statement. The proposed provisions are mostly procedural; including a new no-objection-type procedure which provides that if the Exchange does not object to the transfer within 21 days of receiving the requisite documentation, the transfer may proceed.

D. Incentive Stock Options

If a company proposes to grant directors' and employees' stock options in the private stage and which are to remain outstanding after its prospectus is accepted, then the Superintendent of Brokers, as a matter of practice, adopts the provisions of the Exchange's incentive stock option policy. These provisions are set forth in Exchange Listings Policy Statement No. 1 which is discussed in Chapter 9. Securities Commission Local Policy Statement No. 3-31 (February 1, 1987) is not being applied to the granting of incentive stock options prior to listing on the Exchange.

CHAPTER THREE

Listing Requirements

GENERAL

A. Member Sponsorship

By virtue of Exchange Rule B.1.11.2, every company applying to list its securities on the Exchange must have the listing sponsored by a Member of the Exchange. There are no Exchange rules which impose specific obligations on an Exchange Member in its capacity as sponsor. However, the Exchange considers the role of the sponsoring Member to be an integral part of the listing process, particularly where the sponsoring Member has not acted as the applicant company's underwriter or agent during its initial public offering.

Exchange Listings Policy Statement No. 19 specifically deals with the role of a Member sponsor, both in the case of an initial listing, and in the case of a continued listing where a reverse take-over is involved. Under this Policy Statement, the role of a sponsor primarily involves the Member satisfying itself that the applicant company is a suitable candidate for listing, based on the information made available to the Member. In particular, the Member should consider the composition of the board of directors to ensure that management has the requisite expertise and experience, given the business undertaking of the applicant company, and that the directors are aware of the nature of *(a)* the disclosures required to be made in the listing application and the obligations imposed by the listing agreement, *(b)* the responsibilities they have as directors of a listed company and *(c)* their responsibilities to make accurate and timely disclosure of the company's affairs to the investing public.

If there is no public financing taking place at the time Member sponsorship is required, then in addition to signing the new listing application, the Member must report, by letter to the Exchange, outlining its scope of review of the affairs of the applicant company. Without limiting the scope of inquiry, the areas of review must include the following:

• an interview of management and a review of resumes and any other representations relied on to ensure management and directors are aware of the matters referred to above and will accordingly act in a responsible and capable manner;

- a review of the company's financial position and history by examining financial statements and business plans with a view to establishing a reasonable belief of future profitability or viability of the business undertaking; and
- a review of the Form 4's for all of the directors, a copy of which must be maintained on file with the sponsor. A copy of any directors' and promoters' questionnaire prepared for regulatory purposes is to be similarly reviewed and maintained on file. A sponsor may have its own additional questionnaire to complete for its own information.

The Member should also ensure that the securities of the applicant company which are to be listed are beneficially owned by the required number of public shareholders. Listings Policy Statement No. 19 further provides that the sponsoring Member should be prepared to assist in maintaining an orderly market for the company's securities during the period immediately following listing or the completion of the reverse take-over, particularly where the Member has acted as the applicant company's underwriter or agent during its recent public offering.

B. Pre-Listing Review Committee

At this writing, the Exchange is in the process of forming a Pre-Listing Review Committee consisting of four senior personnel of Members, two non-Member governors of the Exchange, the Exchange's President and one senior official from the Listings Department. The Committee is to do a preliminary review of all companies proposing to list on the Exchange before they file a prospectus and of all companies proposing a reverse take-over. The review will focus on key matters likely to impact the quality of the listing such as the nature of the business, the qualifications of the officers and directors, the major shareholders and the proposed size and method of funding.

The sponsoring Member is to provide the Committee with information in the form of a fact sheet which is to identify the senior officers, directors, professional advisors and greater than 5% shareholders of the applicant company and describe the nature of its business and the terms of the proposed equity financing. The submission will be reviewed and accepted by the Committee prior to the Superintendent of Brokers reviewing any prospectus filing by the applicant company and, if the Committee objects to the applicant company, the Superintendent has indicated that it will not review the prospectus. The sponsoring Member will be responsible for addressing any concern of the Committee.

The requirements of the Pre-Listing Review Committee are to be set out in Exchange Listings Policy Statement No. 19 and are expected to be a substitute for the current requirement of the Member contained in Listings Policy Statement No. 19, specifically, the requirement to report on the Member's scope of review of the applicant company's affairs if no public financing is taking place.

C. Extra-Provincial Company

A company, which has been organized under the laws of a jurisdiction other than British Columbia, applying to list its securities on the Exchange, may have conducted certain transactions which conflict with the securities regulations in British Columbia. For example, the company's conduct of matters discussed in Chapter 2, the sale of seed capital shares, the issuance of shares in consideration for assets and the granting of incentive stock options, may not fit within the parameters established by the Superintendent of Brokers and the Exchange. The Exchange, in Listings Policy Statement No. 18, has stipulated that it will not consider for listing a company, which has entered into transactions within one year from the date of application, which do not comply with the applicable British Columbia securities regulations. This requirement is commonly referred to as the one year listing rule. The applicant company may, however, restructure any such transactions so that they do meet the requirements of the British Columbia securities regulators.

Through Listings Policy Statement No. 18, the Exchange has imposed on applicant companies seeking a listing on the Exchange and which may have conducted recent public offerings outside British Columbia, the same requirements it would have imposed had these companies conducted their public offerings and all other corporate affairs within British Columbia. Given the expectations of the investing public in British Columbia and the large number of listed companies which have conducted their affairs in accordance with applicable British Columbia securities regulations, the Exchange, by having this policy, seeks to ensure compliance with such regulations prior to listing the applicant company's securities.

D. Categorization of Companies

The Exchange has been referred to as a minimum standards exchange since its listing requirements have been minimized to enable start up or junior companies to have their securities traded through its facilities. In response to the varying levels of development of junior companies, the Exchange has established criteria to categorize companies depending on their corporate stature. For listing purposes, a company is categorized by

Part B of Exchange Rule B.1.00 and Listings Policy Statement No. 9, as *(a)* a Venture Company, which is the least developed, *(b)* a Resource or Commercial/Industrial Company, which is partially developed, or *(c)* a Resource or Commercial/Industrial Company with exempt status, which is the most developed. Throughout this book, companies with exempt status will be referred to as exempt companies. The second category of company must meet certain minimum requirements upon listing which are more stringent than for a Venture Company but less stringent than for an exempt company.

The significance of the categorization of companies relates principally to the filing requirements of the Exchange following listing. More advanced companies receive less scrutiny from the Exchange thus, their ongoing filing requirements are less onerous (see Chapter 5).

Listings Policy Statement No. 9 sets out the requirements for Resource or Commercial/Industrial Company designation. This Policy Statement provides that the Exchange will classify companies based on information that is available on the company's file and will make the classification known by public notice and in quotation publications by printing special identifiers beside the company's name. Conversely, pursuant to this Policy Statement, the Exchange may designate a company as a Venture Company where it ceases to meet any of the requirements set out as minimum standards for the Resource or Commercial/Industrial Company categorization. In addition, an applicant company which meets the lowest standards imposed for listing and receives the corresponding designation of a Venture Company may apply to have this designation removed when it fulfills the listing requirements of a Resource or Commercial/Industrial Company.

The Exchange is also permitted, under Part A of Exchange Rule B.1.00, to waive one or more of its listing requirements, when it is satisfied that to do so would not prejudice the public interest. The Exchange is also permitted to impose listing requirements of a more restrictive nature. These powers appear to be used by the Exchange only in isolated instances and where there are valid reasons for doing so. It should be noted that the requirements set out in Listings Policy Statement No. 9 are designed as guidelines only and the Exchange reserves the right to exercise its discretion in applying them.

In summary, to obtain a listing on the Exchange, an applicant company is categorized by the Exchange as a Venture Company or a Resource or Commercial/Industrial Company with or without exempt status. The balance of this Chapter will deal with the listing requirements for a Venture Company, a Resource or Commercial/Industrial Company and an exempt company. The post- listing requirements of the Exchange are discussed in Chapters 5 to 17.

MINIMUM LISTING REQUIREMENTS

Exchange Rule B.1.11 prescribes certain minimum listing requirements for *all* applicant companies regardless of their category. These general requirements are as follows:

- the company must be managed by individuals who have expertise, or the company must have retained a consultant who has expertise, in the area of the company's actual or proposed undertaking;
- the company must be sponsored for listing by a Member;
- the company must have an acceptable registrar and transfer agent in the City of Vancouver;
- the company must have issued at least 500,000 shares under its first prospectus, of which at least 300,000 shares must have been issued to the public. All of these shares must be free of trading restrictions. Shares issued to the public exclude any shares owned by, or issued to, any of the company's insiders;
- the company must be in full compliance with the *Securities Act*, the legislation under which it was incorporated, and any other legislation which may regulate or affect its activities;
- the company must have the lawful right to carry on its actual or proposed business or undertaking;
- a minimum of two signatures must be required on all cheques issued by the company by persons authorized by the board of directors of the company.

The Exchange, in using its discretion to waive listing requirements, generally waives the requirement for two signatures on cheques issued by a Resource or Commercial/Industrial Company, or by an exempt company, and may, depending on the nature of the company's business, waive this requirement for cheques issued below a specified amount.

VENTURE COMPANY

A. General

The minimum listing requirements set out in Exchange Rule B.1.12 must be met by an applicant company in order to be designated a Venture Company and obtain a listing of its securities on the Exchange. These requirements are set out below:

- the company's shares must be beneficially owned by at least 200 shareholders, exclusive of any of the company's insiders, each of whom must beneficially own shares comprising one or more minimum purchase lots free of any trading restrictions. Minimum purchase lots (not to be confused with board lots) are defined as follows:

Public Offering Price	Minimum Purchase Lot
$1.00 or less	1,000
$1.01 to $3.00	500
$3.01 and over	100

- the company must have sufficient funds to carry out the recommended programs of exploration or development work or the funds required under its management plan plus a minimum of $50,000.00 of unallocated funds in the case of a resource company and $100,000.00 in the case of a non-resource company;
- where the applicant company is a resource company, it must have an interest in a natural resource property of potential merit on which the company proposes to conduct recommended exploration or development work. This property must be the subject of a report, prepared by a qualified and independent engineer or geologist, which includes recommendations for the exploration or development work. Where the company is a non-resource company, it must have a management plan covering a period of at least one year for the orderly development of its business or undertaking together with a report detailing the financial requirements of the company for the period covered by the management plan. The Exchange may require this financial report to be prepared by a qualified and independent consultant. Where the company is proposing to develop a product or service, it must provide a feasibility report prepared by a qualified and independent consultant, which specifically details the economic viability of and the demand for the company's proposed product or service. If production of a product is proposed, the company must demonstrate that the product will be capable of being economically produced within the period covered by the management plan.

The word insider, as discussed above, is given the meaning provided for in s.1(1) of the *Securities Act*. Shares are considered to be free of any trading restrictions, for the purposes of the same subparagraph, when they may be transferred at any time to residents of any jurisdiction without limitation. The Exchange does, however, permit the listing of securities with trading restrictions on a special terms market basis. For example, an applicant company's initial public offering may involve securities which may not be resold to United States residents for a certain time period unless certain securities registration requirements in the United States are met. So long as the required number of shareholders beneficially own the requisite number of restricted securities and all other listing requirements are met, the restricted securities may be allowed to trade on the Exchange on the special terms market. The certificates representing the restricted securities must bear a legend disclosing the trading restrictions. The issuance of securities which are subject to trading restrictions and are represented by legended certificates must receive acceptance from the Exchange unless, of course, the trading restrictions are imposed by the Exchange. In giving such acceptance, the Exchange will consider *(a)* the specific wording of the proposed legend, *(b)* the total number of securities issued in the class of securities from which the restricted securities are to be issued, *(c)* the number of restricted securities to be issued and the date the restrictions expire and *(d)* the number of restricted securities previously issued, if any, with details of the legend wording and expiry date of the restrictions. The Exchange may require that acceptance of the legend is subject to establishing a special terms market, which will be determined based on the number of legended shares and the nature of the legend.

B. Special

In the latter part of 1984, the Special Committee, and in the latter part of 1988, the Special Policy Committee, recommended changes to ensure that junior companies conducted their initial public offerings and become listed at a more advanced stage in their economic development and that the initial public offerings were properly distributed to the public. Exchange Rule B.1.13 was introduced and subsequently revised to implement the recommendations of these two Committees through the following special listing requirements:

- prior to the applicant company's first public offering, a minimum of $75,000.00 must have been expended by the applicant company on account of exploration or development work on a company's resource property which is the subject of funding through its public offering and a minimum of $200,000.00 must have been expended on account of business development expenditures in the case of a non-resource company. A minimum of $75,000.00 of the company's first public offering proceeds must be specifically allocated to the properties which the resource company is funding through its public offering;
- the company's seed capital shares must have been sold at not less than $0.25 per share;
- the company must have raised not less than $150,000.00 through the

A board lot refers to a specified number of shares at a specified price per share as set out in Exchange Rule C.1.52. Where a company's shares are trading at less than $1.00 per share, a board lot is comprised of 500 shares and where the shares are trading at $1.00 per share or more, a board lot consists of 100 shares.

B. Resource Company

As set out in Listings Policy Statement No. 9, a Resource Company, meaning a company engaged in the business of exploration and development of natural resource properties, must satisfy the requirements set forth in either 1. or 2. below:

1. • total assets, excluding goodwill, of at least $2,000,000.00;
   • sufficient working capital to carry out any recommended programs of exploration or development plus the greater of $100,000.00 in unallocated funds or sufficient funds to meet estimated general, administrative and capital expenditures for a period of 18 months; and
   • an interest in a property of demonstrable merit with potential economic value. In the case of a mineral property, the company should have performed extensive exploration or development work on the property and the property should be the subject of further proposed exploration or development work in accordance with recommendations made in a report by a qualified independent engineer or geologist. This report should recommend at least $400,000.00 to be spent in the next phase of exploration or development. In the case of a property containing hydrocarbons, the property should be generating sufficient cash flow to the company to pay the company's cost of acquiring and developing the property and to generate a profit to the company within a five year period of the completion of the well or wells. Alternatively, the property should contain proven reserves of recoverable oil or gas, as calculated by a qualified independent petroleum consultant, that are capable of producing such cash flow; or

2. • a mineral property with proven reserves for a three year mine life upon which an acceptable program of additional exploration or development work sufficient to develop further reserves is proposed; and
   • adequate working capital to carry on the business.

31

C. Commercial/Industrial Company

As set out in Listings Policy Statement No. 9, a Commercial/Industrial Company, which is a company engaged in a business other than the exploration and development of natural resource properties, must satisfy the requirements set forth in either 1. or 2. below:

1. • total assets of at least $1,000,000.00;
    • a service which it can provide or a product which it can produce on a commercial and sustained basis. The company should have a business plan acceptable to the Exchange which must cover a period of at least one year, respecting the continued development of its business or undertaking. Should the business plan include forecast financial statements, they must be prepared in accordance with guidelines established by The Canadian Institute of Chartered Accountants and which detail the financial requirements of the company for the first year of the period covered by the business plan;
    • earned operating revenue in the immediately preceding fiscal year; and
    • sufficient working capital to satisfy the financial requirements of its business plan plus the greater of $200,000.00 in unallocated funds or sufficient funds to meet estimated general, administrative and capital expenditures for a period of two years; or

2. • earnings of at least $100,000.00 before taxes, in the immediately preceding fiscal year;
    • pre-tax cash flow of at least $300,000.00 in the immediately preceding fiscal year;
    • a business plan which must cover a period of at least one year, respecting the continued development of its business or undertaking which may include forecast financial statements prepared in accordance with the guidelines established by The Canadian Institute of Chartered Accountants; and
    • sufficient working capital to satisfy the financial requirements of its business plan.

EXEMPT STATUS

A. Resource-Exempt Company

In addition to satisfying the Resource Company requirements, a

Resource Company with exempt status must satisfy each of the following as provided for in Listings Policy Statement No. 9:

- pre-tax profitability in the immediately preceding fiscal year;
- pre-tax cash flow of $350,000.00 in the immediately preceding fiscal year and an average annual pre-tax cash flow of $300,000.00 for the two immediately preceding fiscal years;
- in the case of an oil and gas company, proven reserves of recoverable oil and gas having a value of at least $3,500,000.00 based on the discount rate prescribed by the Exchange, or in the case of a mining company, proven reserves of ore sufficient to yield a mine life of at least five years; and
- adequate working capital to carry on its business.

B. Commercial/Industrial-Exempt Company

In addition to satisfying the Commercial/Industrial Company requirements, a Commercial/Industrial Company with exempt status must satisfy each of the following as set out in Listings Policy Statement No. 9:

- net tangible assets (which may include deferred development charges or other intangible assets if, in the opinion of the Exchange, the circumstances warrant such inclusion) having a value of at least $3,500,000.00;
- pre-tax profitability in the immediately preceding fiscal year;
- an average annual pre-tax cash flow of $300,000.00 for the two immediately preceding fiscal years; and
- adequate working capital to carry on its business.

CHAPTER FOUR

Listing Procedures

GENERAL

The Rules of the Exchange provide for three types of listing applications, each type involving a distinct procedure and specified documentation. The type of listing application used by an applicant company will depend on when the company has completed a public offering and, if a public offering has never been conducted, the jurisdiction in which the public offering is proposed.

The three types of listing applications are referred to as *(a)* the standard form listing application, *(b)* the wrap-around listing application and *(c)* the conditional listing application.

The standard form application is used by an applicant company which has not completed a public offering within 60 days of the listing application and the wrap-around application is used where an applicant company has completed a public offering within this period. Where an applicant company is proposing to conduct its first public offering in British Columbia pursuant to an underwriting agreement or a fixed price agency agreement (described later in this Chapter), the conditional listing application may be used, permitting the public offering to be conducted through the facilities of the Exchange.

Part A of Exchange Rule B.1.00 provides that, where a listing application is accepted by the Exchange, the securities of the applicant company will be listed and posted for trading at a time set by the Exchange. On the trading day prior to the actual listing, the Exchange will issue an Exchange Notice advising of the new listing and will print, at the expense of the company, a complete copy of the company's listing application for distribution to its subscribers. The listed company must, unless exempted, comply with all the terms of the listing agreement, all the terms of any other agreement providing for the consent or prior acceptance of the Exchange (such as stock options, share purchase warrants, escrow or pooling restrictions), all applicable By-laws, Rules and Listings Policy Statements of the Exchange and any direction, decision, order or ruling made by the Exchange pursuant to any such agreements, By-laws, Rules or Listings Policy Statements.

All listing applications and supporting documentation, as well as the prescribed fees, become the property of the Exchange and may be retained by the Exchange even if the applications are refused. Once a listing application has been filed, the applicant company may be permitted, on terms imposed by the Exchange, to withdraw or amend the application.

In the case of the standard form and wrap-around applications, the listing procedures and required documentation are set out in Exchange Rule B.1.00 and the listing application forms. Exchange Rule B.5.00 provides for the conditional listing process. The balance of this Chapter deals with the methods of applying for listing on the Exchange and the circumstances under which a listing may be refused. As well, the method of obtaining a listing by acquiring an already listed company, referred to as a reverse take-over or back door listing, will be discussed as an alternative to the direct listing of a company's securities.

STANDARD FORM LISTING APPLICATION

A. General

The standard form application process is commonly used by companies which have become public companies outside of British Columbia and which have been public for a period of at least one year prior to their listing application (to avoid the one year listing rule). The standard form application differs significantly in two ways from the other two methods of application. It involves the applicant company completing a questionnaire in narrative form disclosing all relevant corporate material facts. This information, in the case of the wrap-around and conditional listing applications, is contained in the applicant company's prospectus or public offering document which forms part of the listing application. Because the wrap-around and conditional listing applications involve a public offering document which has been reviewed in detail by the Superintendent of Brokers or similar regulatory authority, the review process by the Exchange is limited. With the standard form application, the Exchange's review is more extensive since it is the only regulatory body examining the company's affairs.

B. Procedure

Listing applicants using the standard form application are required to use the same procedure, whether they be Venture Companies, Resource or Commercial/Industrial Companies, or exempt companies. Following preparation and execution of the relevant documentation, it is filed with the

Listings Department of the Exchange. The Exchange is primarily concerned with ensuring that the applicant company meets all of the listing requirements applicable to it. Any questions or comments which the Exchange has on the filed documentation (referred to as "deficiencies"), will be communicated to the company and its filing solicitor. The deficiencies must be dealt with to the satisfaction of the Exchange before it will accept the listing application for filing as well as list and post the securities of the applicant company for trading on the Exchange.

Securities Commission Local Policy Statement No. 3-19 (February 1, 1987) requires the filing of certain documentation with the Superintendent of Brokers at the same time a listing application is filed with the Exchange. The Superintendent does not issue formal written consent to the application, however, the Exchange will generally ensure that the Superintendent has no objection to the listing prior to approving the application. Local Policy Statement No. 3-19 provides that the Superintendent must notify the applicant company and the Exchange within seven working days of receiving the listing documentation where the Superintendent considers remedial measures are required. The Securities Commission retains the right, pursuant to Local Policy Statement No. 3-19, to prohibit any company from listing its securities on the Exchange. The grounds on which the Securities Commission will object to a listing are set out in Local Policy Statement No. 3-19 and will be discussed later in this Chapter.

C. Documentation Requirements

The documents required to be filed in support of a standard form listing application are more extensive for Venture and Resource or Commercial/Industrial Companies than for exempt companies. The main document is the listing application form which involves answering, in narrative form, 25 questions in the case of a Venture Company or a Resource or Commercial/Industrial Company and seven questions in the case of an exempt company. An exempt company must respond to queries such as the location of its offices, particulars of its authorized and issued share capital, listings on other stock exchanges and the dates of certain financial statements and public offering documents.

In support of the application, an exempt company must submit the applicable listing fee and file with the Exchange a copy of its last annual report (including audited financial statements) sent to shareholders and its latest interim financial statements, a copy of any prospectus or other similar offering document filed with any securities regulatory authority within the past twelve months, a copy of any recent listing application on another stock exchange and specimen certificates of shares or other securities to be listed.

The listing application for a Venture Company or a Resource or Commercial/Industrial Company calls for detailed disclosure similar to that contained in a prospectus and, accordingly, its preparation is time consuming. Much of the information to be provided is historical, informing the Exchange of the company's prior affairs. In addition to the standard form listing application and the prescribed listing fee, a Venture Company or a Resource or Commercial/Industrial Company must file the following supporting documentation with the Exchange, as required by the listing application form:

- its most recent prospectus together with amendments, if any, and a copy of each letter of acceptance from the applicable securities regulatory authorities;
- a government certificate or legal opinion evidencing that the company is in good standing;
- a schedule of all properties held setting out legal descriptions, interests held and details of all encumbrances. The schedule must be accompanied by a sworn declaration of the directors attesting to its content;
- if the company is a resource company, a report for each of its major properties must be prepared by a qualified and independent engineer or geologist. This report must include recommendations for exploration or development work. If the company is a non-resource company, it must submit a management plan, a report detailing its financial requirements for the period covered by the plan and, if required, a technical report, prepared by a qualified and independent consultant, detailing the demand for and the economic viability of the company's proposed product or service;
- audited financial statements for the most recently completed financial year and the latest interim financial statements sent to shareholders;
- copies of all agreements under which shares have been issued for other than cash during the past twelve months and copies of all agreements which provide for the issuance of shares subsequent to listing;
- copies of all agreements covering stock options, share purchase warrants, escrow and pooling restrictions and voting trusts. The escrow and pooling agreements should provide for the jurisdiction of the Exchange;
- copies of all management or employment agreements;
- a specimen share certificate;
- a current list of registered shareholders certified by the company's registrar and transfer agent;
- an executed listing agreement and statutory declaration; and
- a copy of the directors' resolution authorizing the deponent director(s)

to execute the listing agreement and the statutory declaration.

Copies of all documents must be certified as true copies of the originals. The Exchange may also require additional material and information.

There is no difference in the documentation to be filed by an applicant company, in any Exchange category, with the Superintendent of Brokers contemporaneously with the listing application to the Exchange. However, it does vary if the Superintendent has ever issued a receipt for a prospectus of the company and the receipt was issued within twelve months of the listing application.

Where an application to list is made within twelve months of the date on which a prospectus, receipted by the Superintendent, was certified by the company's directors, the company need only file a copy of its listing application with the Superintendent. If more than twelve months have elapsed, in addition to a copy of the listing application, an affirmation must be filed affirming that;

- a Form 4 has been filed by each current and proposed director within a three year period preceding the date of application;
- insider reports (prescribed forms under the Securities Act) have been filed up-to-date by each current and proposed director;
- the company is in good standing with the Registrar of Companies or similar authority in the relevant jurisdiction; and
- the company is up-to-date with any filings which may be required by legislation.

If the Superintendent of Brokers has never issued a receipt for a prospectus of the applicant company, the company must provide the Superintendent with the affirmation described above and copies of the listing application, the most recent annual audited financial statements and interim financial statements distributed to shareholders and the most recent prospectus accepted in a securities jurisdiction other than British Columbia. As well, if the applicant company has not made a distribution of its securities by way of a public offering document in any securities jurisdiction, the Superintendent must be given an explanation or description of the means by which the distribution to shareholders was achieved.

WRAP-AROUND LISTING APPLICATION

A. General

The wrap-around listing application was most commonly used by companies which had conducted their public offerings in British Columbia other than pursuant to an underwriting agreement or the type of agency agreement which would permit a conditional listing. However, a notice of the Securities Commission (April 5, 1989) indicates that the Superintendent of Brokers generally will not issue a receipt for a prospectus offering of securities of a junior resource or industrial company where an application for conditional listing on a Canadian stock has not been made. The net effect of this notice is that prospectus offerings in British Columbia will require the conditional listing procedure to be used. The wrap-around application may be used by companies which have conducted public offerings outside of British Columbia. The application must be made within 60 days of completing the public offering. Since the Superintendent of Brokers or a similar regulatory authority will have recently reviewed the company's affairs disclosed in the prospectus or other public offering document, the Exchange's scrutiny is generally limited to ensuring that its minimum listing requirements are satisfied and, in the case of companies which have conducted their offerings outside British Columbia, that their transactions comply with British Columbia securities regulations in accordance with the one year listing rule.

B. Procedure

The review by the Exchange of the wrap-around listing application is tied to obtaining regulatory approval to the applicant company's public offering document and the subsequent completion of the public offering. The procedure for listing Venture Companies, Resource or Commercial/Industrial Companies, and exempt companies is the same with the wrap-around application process.

Following preparation of the listing documentation and the acceptance of the applicant company's prospectus, the company may file part of the listing documentation (as described below) with the Exchange which is then reviewed by the Exchange. Any comments which the Exchange may have respecting the filed material must be responded to either before or after the company's public offering is conducted. Upon completion of the company's public offering, the company files the remaining listing documentation described below. If such documentation is acceptable to the Exchange, the Exchange will approve the listing of the company's securities on the Exchange. The applicant company may choose to file all listing documentation after the company's public offering is conducted.

The approval process of the Superintendent of Brokers regarding a wrap-around application is the same as that of a standard form application. Specifically, the Superintendent does not formally approve the application in writing, however, if the Superintendent considers remedial measures are required, the company and the Exchange must be notified within the specified time. As well, the Securities Commission has the authority to prohibit the listing in the circumstances described later in this Chapter.

C. Documentation Requirements

Exchange Rule B.1.02 sets out the documents required to be filed with the Exchange for a wrap-around listing application. Information and material in addition to that set out in Rule B.1.02 may be required by the Exchange. The Exchange generally does not require all of the documentation set out in Exchange Rule B.1.02 for an exempt company, whose filings will be dealt with on a case-by-case basis.

In the wrap-around listing process, an applicant company's prospectus forms the disclosure base of the company's material facts and, accordingly, the application is "wrapped around" the prospectus. Following acceptance of the company's prospectus by the applicable regulatory authority and before the public offering is conducted, the following documents may be filed with the Exchange with the prescribed listing fee:

- certified copies of the prospectus (and any amendments thereto), the regulatory authority's acceptance of the prospectus, any other prospectus or similar securities offering document issued by the company in the year preceding the application date and the acceptance letters for same;
- certified copies of all agreements requiring or providing for the pooling, escrowing, holding, voting, allotment or issuance of the company's securities;
- certified copies of all agreements made, directly or indirectly, between the company, its management or its insiders;
- an affidavit sworn by each director of the company attesting to the legal description of the company's property, the company's interest therein and particulars of any encumbrances, whether registered or unregistered, against the said property;
- a copy of the directors' resolution authorizing the deponent director(s). to execute the listing agreement and statutory declaration;
- a government certificate or legal opinion evidencing the company is in good standing;
- any engineering reports, management plans, financial reports or other reports required by Exchange Rule B.1.00 to satisfy the minimum listing requirements;
- a copy of the company's constating documents; and
- a specimen share certificate and share purchase warrant certificate (if applicable) with the CUSIP number printed thereon.

After the applicant company's public offering is completed, the above documentation, if not filed following acceptance of the company's prospectus, must be filed with the Exchange with the following documents:

- an executed listing agreement and statutory declaration;
- an affidavit sworn by each director of the company attesting to any material changes which would make untrue or misleading any statement of material facts contained in the prospectus (and any amendments thereto); and
- a list of the names and addresses of the company's shareholders.

Where the applicant company's prospectus was certified by its directors within one year of the wrap-around listing application, the company need only file a copy of its listing application with the Superintendent of Brokers at the same time it is filed with the Exchange. In any other case, the filings required by the Superintendent are the same as those required with a standard form application.

CONDITIONAL LISTING APPLICATION

A. General

The conditional listing application is made to the Exchange at the same time an applicant company files its preliminary prospectus with the Superintendent of Brokers. This application results in the conditional listing of the company's securities contemporaneously with a receipt being issued by the Superintendent for the company's final prospectus. The listing is conditional until the company has satisfied the Exchange that it has met the distribution requirements and the financial requirements imposed by Exchange Rule B.1.00, specifically, that it has the required number of public shareholders and the requisite amount of money to provide for its planned expenditures and for working capital. Such requirements should be fulfilled once the company completes its public offering pursuant to its prospectus. Following the public offering, which will be conducted through the facilities of the Exchange, the conditional listing may be removed and the company's securities listed, posted and called for trading on the Exchange. The conditional listing application may be used, however, only where the public offering involves an underwriting agreement or fixed price agency agreement as will be described later in this Chapter.

The conditional listing and the subsequent public offering and posting of the company's securities for trading on the Exchange are referred to as the Initial Distribution System and are regulated by Exchange Rule B.5.00. The

Initial Distribution System is considered the quickest and most efficient way of obtaining a listing on the Exchange.

The following discussion does not deal with the qualification of the applicant company's prospectus in jurisdictions outside of British Columbia nor with the matter of prospectus preparation, the content of the prospectus and the nature of the supporting documentation required by the Superintendent of Brokers, all of which are beyond the scope of this book. The following discussion will be limited to the procedure involved in the Initial Distribution System and the documentation requirements of the Exchange, only.

B. Procedure

The review by the Superintendent of Brokers and the Exchange of the prospectus and listing application are concurrent since the public offering under the prospectus will be conducted through the facilities of the Exchange and the company's securities will be listed soon after this takes place. The review by each regulatory authority will focus on different aspects of the applicant company. Generally, the Superintendent will be concerned with corporate matters of the company, particularly, share issuances and the consideration received by the company for those shares, the proposed use of proceeds from the public offering and the suitability of the company's management. The Exchange primarily will be concerned with ensuring that the public offering will be conducted in accordance with the rules of the Exchange and that the applicant company may, if the offering is completed, meet the minimum listing requirements of the Exchange.

The applicant company's preliminary prospectus, required under s.42 of the *Securities Act*, must be prepared in accordance with the *Act*. The company files with the Superintendent its preliminary prospectus and a number of additional documents as set out in Securities Commission Local Policy Statement No. 3-02 (January 20, 1989). At the same time, an application is made to the Exchange for a conditional listing by way of an initial filing (as described below). The Superintendent issues a receipt for the company's preliminary prospectus, and, subsequently, both the Superintendent and the Exchange review the filings and communicate any deficiencies to the filing solicitor and the applicant company's underwriter or agent. The deficiencies must then be cured and the responses filed with the Superintendent and the Exchange along with a draft of the final prospectus. Assuming that any further deficiencies are dealt with to the satisfaction of the Superintendent and the Exchange, the company files its final prospectus and certain documents as set out in Local Policy Statement No. 3-02 with the Superintendent and the Exchange and the Superintendent issues a receipt for the prospectus. The Exchange conditionally lists the company's securities on the Exchange (but does not post or call the securities for trading) effective on the date of the Superintendent of Brokers' receipt. The Exchange then must notify its Members of the conditional listing by issuing an Exchange Notice. The applicant company must make a second filing, described below, with the Exchange following the conditional listing.

Pursuant to Exchange Rule B.5.00, the applicant company's initial public offering or initial distribution through the facilities of the Exchange must occur within 180 calendar days of the conditional listing, which period cannot be extended. The offering must be conducted on a particular day, known as the offering day, which is determined by the underwriter or agent and the applicant company, with the Exchange's consent. The Exchange must be notified of the offering day no later than 11:00 a.m. on the trading day preceding the offering day so that it may issue an Exchange Notice to its Members of the initial distribution. The company must deliver to the Exchange at least 50 copies of its final prospectus, not later than 11:00 a.m. on the trading day preceding the offering day and at least 240 copies not later than 9:00 a.m. on the offering day. The number of copies may vary depending on the Exchange's needs.

The initial distribution is effected by the underwriter or agent crossing the company's securities, either from its own account to clients' accounts (in an underwriting) or from the company's account to clients' accounts (in a fixed price agency offering) on the trading floor of the Exchange on the offering day. The underwriter or agent is not required to make any of the offering available to other Members of the Exchange.

Following the offering day, the underwriter or agent and the company must make a final filing, described below, with the Exchange; the filing required from the underwriter or agent must be made within five business days of the offering day. Following a review of the final filing by the Exchange to ensure that all listing requirements are satisfied, the company's securities will be listed, posted and called for trading on the Exchange. Exchange Listings Policy Statement No. 15 provides that, if the final filing is made with the Exchange before 9:00 a.m. on the offering day, the company's securities may be listed, posted and called for trading at 10:00 a.m. on the offering day. The Exchange should be advised by not later than 11:00 a.m. on the trading day immediately preceding the offering day that the company wishes to have its securities called for trading by 10:00 a.m. on the offering day.

C. Documentation Requirements

The documentation required for a conditional listing application is set out in Exchange Rule B.5.00. The initial filing with the Exchange, which is made concurrently with the filing of the preliminary prospectus and supporting documentation with the Superintendent of Brokers, consists of the following documents:

- a copy of the company's submission letter to the Superintendent and a copy of the preliminary prospectus (including all financial statements, technical reports and other documents which form part of the prospectus). The preliminary prospectus must refer to the company's application to conditionally list its securities; and
- a draft of the underwriting agreement or fixed price agency offering agreement respecting the company's initial public offering.

The listing fee and the fee for the proposed public offering also must be provided with the initial filing. The Exchange may require that other documentation be filed at this time. For example, a list of the current shareholders of the company and copies of any agreements regarding management remuneration or transactions with insiders may be requested. In any event, a fully executed underwriting or agency agreement must be delivered to the Exchange prior to the conditional listing.

The second filing, which is made immediately following the conditional listing and issuance of the Superintendent of Brokers' receipt for the final prospectus, consists of the following documents:

- a certified copy of the Superintendent of Brokers' receipt for the final prospectus;
- a statutory declaration and executed listing application with a copy of the final prospectus attached (including all financial statements, technical reports and other documents which form a part of the prospectus). The final prospectus must refer to the conditional listing of the company's securities;
- certified copies of all agreements requiring or providing for the pooling, escrowing, holding, voting, allotment or issuance of any of the company's securities;
- certified copies of all agreements made, directly or indirectly, between the company and its insiders;
- a specimen share certificate and share purchase warrant certificate (if applicable) with the CUSIP number printed thereon;
- a list, certified by the company's registrar and transfer agent, of the company's shareholders;
- a copy of the directors' resolution authorizing the deponent director(s) to execute the listing agreement and statutory declaration;
- any engineering reports, management plans, financial reports or other reports, as may be required by Exchange Rule B.1.00 to satisfy the minimum listing requirements;
- a copy of the company's constating documents; and
- a completed data questionnaire form as prescribed by the Exchange.

The final filing must be submitted in order to remove the conditional listing and have the company's securities listed, posted and called for trading and consists of the following documents:

- a list, which must be submitted within five business days of the initial public offering, provided by the underwriter or agent showing the names and addresses of the beneficial purchasers of the company's securities together with the number of securities purchased by each; and
- a declaration from each director filed by the company and not to be dated before the offering day, stating that there have been no material changes that would make untrue or misleading any statement of material facts contained in the company's prospectus or, if such a change has occurred, the particulars of the material change and a copy of the company's prospectus amendment.

The company need not make any additional filings with the Superintendent of Brokers prior to proceeding with a listing on the Exchange.

Exchange Rule B.5.08 provides the Exchange with the power to revoke a conditional listing, refuse to list the company's securities for trading and cancel the trades comprising the initial distribution, when the Exchange is of the opinion that the listing requirements provided for in Exchange Rule B.1.00 have not been satisfied. Where the Exchange refuses to list, post and call for trading the company's securities, it must notify its Members by issuing an Exchange Notice.

D. Types of Initial Distributions

As discussed above, the conditional listing application may be made only if the applicant company has arranged for its initial distribution pursuant to an underwriting agreement or fixed price agency offering agreement. An underwriting involves the direct purchase of the company's securities by the underwriter who, in turn, sells them to the public through the facilities of the Exchange. The underwriter buys the securities at a price discounted from the price paid for those securities by the public. In an agency offering, the company's securities are sold to the public through the facilities of the Exchange by a Member of the Exchange who acts as agent for the company. The agent receives a commission, a percentage of the gross proceeds of the offering, for acting as agent.

The initial distribution, by way of an underwriting or fixed price agency offering, has minimum requirements imposed by Exchange Rule B.5.00, for the offering both of shares and units.

One of the fundamental differences between an underwriting and a fixed price agency offering relates to the time the securities are paid for. Underwriting proceeds must be paid to the company within ten business days of the date the Superintendent of Brokers issues a receipt for the company's prospectus. The net proceeds from the agency offering must be paid within ten business days of the offering day; this may occur at any time within 180 calendar days of the date a receipt was issued for the prospectus. As well, the underwriter does not have the opportunity to terminate or market out of the underwriting agreement after a receipt is issued for the prospectus. In a fixed price agency offering, the agency agreement generally provides the agent with the opportunity to market out at any time prior to and after the offering day but before the company's securities are posted and called for trading on the Exchange, therefore, the approval of the prospectus does not ensure that the company's securities will be sold.

An underwriter or agent must not assign any underwriting, option or agency agreement nor enter into any sub-underwriting, sub-option or sub-agency agreement unless the Exchange has given its prior approval. However, an underwriter or agent may offer selling group participation in the normal course of the brokerage business to selling groups of other licenced dealers, brokers and investment dealers provided disclosure is made in the company's prospectus.

Exchange Rule B.1.13 provides that the net proceeds to an applicant company from an initial distribution, when combined with the net proceeds received from the sale of its seed capital shares, must be not less than $350,000.00 in the case of a resource company and not less than $625,000.00 in the case of a non-resource company. While the public offering price of the shares or units is negotiated between the company and the underwriter or agent, the minimum net price to the company from the sale of shares must be $0.30 per share and the minimum net price to the company from the sale of units must be $0.40 per unit unless the unit is comprised of more than one share in which case the minimum net price must be the product of $0.40 multiplied by the number of shares comprising the unit. Exchange Rule B.5.00 provides that not less than 500,000 shares must be sold in a share offering and the units sold in a unit offering must be comprised of at least 500,000 shares and at least 300,000 share purchase warrants.

Whether the share purchase warrants in a unit offering are transferable or non-transferable, the total number of shares which may be issued on exercise of the warrants must not exceed the total number of shares issued as part of the unit offering. The exercise of the warrants must not entitle the holder to acquire further warrants, which are referred to as piggyback warrants. The term of the warrants must not exceed two years commencing on the date the company's securities are listed and posted for trading. The exercise price of the warrants is determined by the company and the underwriter or agent and must, in the first year of the warrant term, be at least equal to the price per share and for the second year of the term be increased by at least 15% of the price per share. The price per share in computed by dividing the unit price by the number of shares comprising the unit.

Subject to filing proof with the Exchange that not less than 40 persons, including Members, hold transferable share purchase warrants, the warrants may be posted for trading on the Exchange. If the warrants are exercised to the extent that the Exchange is of the opinion that there is insufficient distribution thereof for an orderly market, the warrants may be traded on a cash basis, and the purchaser of the warrants must pay for the warrants on the same day the purchase is made rather than within the normal five day settlement period. Where the number of warrants outstanding is reduced to less than 75,000, the warrants will be delisted from the Exchange. In any event, during the last six trading days, the warrants will only trade for cash.

Transferable share purchase warrants may be issued in bearer form and the non-transferable share purchase warrants must be issued in the name of the holder and have the words non- transferable displayed prominently on the warrant certificate.

E. Broker's Compensation

The compensation payable to an underwriter or an agent involved in an initial distribution is regulated by Exchange Rule B.5.00. In November, 1988, the Exchange amended Rule B.5.00 to rescind the restrictions governing maximum discounts and commissions which could be charged by Members involved in an initial distribution. An applicant company is now free to sell its shares or units to an underwriter at a price negotiated between the company and the underwriter and to pay a negotiated commission to an agent for a fixed price agency offering.

An applicant company is permitted to grant options to an underwriter for underwriting the company's securities, whereas an agent in a fixed price agency offering is not entitled to any compensation, other than a commission, unless the agent guarantees to purchase the company's securities which are not subscribed for on the day the securities of the company are listed and posted for trading on the Exchange. In consideration for the guarantee, the company may grant a non-transferable share purchase warrant to the agent.

The number of shares which may be acquired pursuant to the exercise of an underwriter's option or an agent's warrant granted in connection with an initial distribution must not be more than 25% of the number of shares in the public offering where the public offering price is less than or equal to $1.00, and not more than 50% of the number of shares in the public offering where the public offering price is greater than $1.00. The maximum term for exercise of an underwriter's option or an agent's warrant is two years. Where the initial distribution involves an offering of units, the term of an agent's warrant must not exceed the term of the public's share purchase warrants.

In the case of an underwriter's option, the exercise price per share in the first year of the option period must be at least equal to the underwriting price and in the second year of the option period must be increased by not less than 15% of the underwriting price. The exercise price of an agent's warrant in the first year of the warrant term must be at least equal to the public offering price and in the second year of the warrant term must be increased by not less than 15% of the public offering price. In the case of a unit offering, the exercise price of an agent's warrant must not be less than the exercise price of the public's share purchase warrants. An underwriter or agent may transfer an interest in the option or warrant to a sub-underwriter or a sub-agent who is part of a selling group participating in the public offering.

The shares acquired pursuant to the exercise, in whole or in part, of an underwriter's option or an agent's warrant may form a part of the initial distribution provided that (a) the trades are effected on the trading floor of the Exchange as part of the initial distribution, (b) all shares so acquired are sold at the same price and (c) the shares are sold at a price equal to or exceeding the exercise price of the option or warrant. The underwriter or agent must advise the Exchange of the exercise of the option or warrant and the number of such shares which will form part of the initial distribution, by not later than 11:00 a.m. on the trading day immediately preceding the day on which the Exchange lists, posts and calls for trading the company's securities.

It should be noted that, pursuant to the recommendations of the Special Committee, the Superintendent of Brokers revised certain regulatory policies to ensure that underwriters and agents and their associates do not compete with the investing public insofar as the selling of seed capital shares is concerned and to restrict the number of such shares which underwriters, agents and their associates can acquire. The Special Policy Committee has made further recommendations in this regard (as discussed in Chapter 2).

F. Greenshoe Options

In the case of an initial distribution, a greenshoe option may be granted to an underwriter or an agent to purchase additional securities of the applicant company. The greenshoe option may be exercised at the conclusion of the initial distribution to provide additional shares or units to the market where the offering has been over-subscribed, thereby facilitating stability in the secondary trading market of the company's securities.

The requirements in respect of the greenshoe option are set out in Exchange Rule B.5.00. The maximum number of securities which may be acquired on the exercise of the greenshoe option is the lesser of *(a)* 15% of the number of shares or units sold to the public and *(b)* the actual number of shares or units sold by the underwriter or agent by way of over-subscription. The number of securities over-subscribed must be determined, and the Exchange must be notified of the over-subscription, not later than 5 days after the offering day, excluding any non-trading days, but prior to the full listing day. The maximum term of the greenshoe option must not exceed 60 calendar days from the day on which the company's shares are fully listed. The exercise price of the option must be the same as the net price received by the company from the sale of its shares or units pursuant to the initial distribution.

LISTING REFUSAL

Exchange Rule B.1.04 provides that the Exchange may refuse to accept a listing application if it is satisfied that to do so would be in the public interest. Such refusal is subject to the right of appeal, by way of a hearing and review, under Part 17 of the *Securities Act*.

In the Matter of Mariah Resources Ltd., Corporate and Financial Services Commission (December 21, 1984), involved an appeal from the Exchange's refusal to accept the conditional listing application of Mariah Resources Ltd. (Mariah). Mariah had entered into an agreement with a Mr. Dennis Johnson to acquire a resource property interest in consideration of certain cash and shares of Mariah. Mr. Johnson, through his associates, had also purchased seed capital shares of Mariah. Mr. Johnson was a stock broker with a brokerage firm in the United States which was not a Member of the Exchange. Mr. Johnson was not registered as a salesman under the former *Act* nor was he a registered representative as was then defined in the Rules of the Exchange.

Certain Rules of the Exchange prohibit a registered representative from receiving any compensation in respect of the sale of any property interest to a company listed on the Exchange, without the prior approval of the Exchange (see Chapter 12). The policies of the Superintendent of Brokers restrict the number of seed capital shares which a salesman may purchase in a company and also deal with the continued fitness for registration of a salesman who sells a property interest to a listed or unlisted company. The Exchange refused to accept the conditional listing application of Mariah on the grounds that it would be in the public interest to apply these policies of sale of seed capital shares in the case of a resource company and $275,000.00 in the case of non-resource companies;

- the net price to the company from the sale of securities during its initial public offering must have been not less than $0.30 per share (in the case of a share offering) or $0.40 per unit (in the case of a unit offering);
- the combined net proceeds to the company from the sale of its seed capital shares and from its initial public offering must have been not less than $350,000.00 for a resource company and $625,000.00 for a non-resource company;
- where the company's initial public offering was conducted within one year of the date of its listing application, the offering must have been effected other than pursuant to a security issuer's licence issued under the *Securities Act* or other similar licences issued pursuant to other securities legislation, unless special circumstances existed; and
- the transfer of any of a listed company's escrow or pooled shares will not be consented to by the Exchange for a period of one year after its securities are listed on the Exchange, except in the case of a *bona fide* transfer of a portion of the shares, unless all of the specifically allocated proceeds disclosed in the company's prospectus have been so expended.

The provisions of paragraph 13(2)(f) of the *Regulation to the Securities Act* permit a company to apply for a security issuer licence which enables any of its directors who are registered under the *Act* to sell securities comprising the company's first public offering directly to the public. The Special Committee, as part of its study, concluded that a significant number of public offerings conducted under security issuer licences were not properly or adequately distributed to the public and it accordingly recommended to the Superintendent of Brokers that a moratorium be declared respecting the issuance of future security issuer licences.

RESOURCE OR COMMERCIAL/INDUSTRIAL COMPANY

A. General

As set out in Listings Policy Statement No. 9, the only general minimum listing requirement which applies to both a Resource or Commercial/Industrial Company relates to the public distribution and to its market capitalization. A Resource or Commercial/Industrial Company must have a market capitalization of at least $700,000.00 (excluding escrow shares) and at least 1,000,000 free-trading shares held by at least 300 public shareholders, each holding one board lot or more.

the Exchange and the Superintendent to stock brokers whether they were stock brokers with Members of the Exchange or otherwise.

The Commission, in considering the matter, stated that no corporation has any legal right to have any of its securities listed on the Exchange and that given the present state of the law, the Exchange is free to accept or reject listing applications as it sees fit. The Commission pointed out it was the Exchange's Rules which made the public interest the sole criteria to be applied when a listing application was being considered.

The Commission held the further view that, in deciding on the acceptance or refusal of a listing, the decision of the Exchange as to what is or is not in the public interest is one with which the Commission will not interfere unless it feels the Exchange to be clearly wrong. The Commission found that there was no suggestion that the Exchange refused Mariah's listing application capriciously, frivolously or in bad faith and the appeal was dismissed.

Under Securities Commission Local Policy Statement No. 3-19 (February 1, 1987), the Securities Commission retains the right to prohibit an applicant company from listing its securities on the Exchange and will prohibit a listing when any one of the following conditions occur:

- the company is engaged in a primary distribution under a prospectus other than a distribution of outstanding agent's warrants or underwriter's options;
- the company is not in full compliance with the *Company Act* and the *Securities Act*;
- the company seeking a listing after being designated dormant has failed to seek reinstatement in accordance with Local Policy Statement No. 3-35 (October 13, 1989);
- the company does not appear to comply with the guidelines set out in the Rules and Listings Policy Statements of the Exchange;
- the company has not made a public offering by way of prospectus in any securities jurisdiction and fails to satisfy the Superintendent of Brokers that the existing distribution of shares and the information on the business and affairs of the company available to the public will suffice to develop an efficient market for the company's shares; or
- the company, subsequent to the conclusion of a public offering, has incurred or initiated any of the following changes in its affairs without prior discussion with the Superintendent of Brokers: *(a)* actual or proposed changes in control of the company, *(b)* actual or proposed acquisitions or dispositions of material assets, *(c)* proposed take-overs, mergers, consolidations, amalgamations or reorganizations, or *(d)* proposed changes in capital structure including conversions, stock consolidations, stock splits or stock dividends.

This list is not intended to be exhaustive and, accordingly, the Securities Commission may find other grounds on which to prohibit a listing.

REVERSE TAKE-OVERS

The reactivation of an inactive or dormant company listed on the Exchange often involves the acquisition of assets, such as all of the outstanding shares of a private company, for shares of the listed company. Where, as a consequence of such a transaction, or series of related transactions, *(a)* new shareholders will own more than 50% of the voting shares of the listed company through newly issued treasury shares or a transfer or purchase of existing voting shares or *(b)* there is an increase of 50% of the issued share capital of the listed company accompanied by a substantial management change or a change in the listed company's undertaking which is deemed by the Exchange to be a reverse take-over, the transaction will involve a reverse take-over as defined by Exchange Listings Policy Statement No. 22. In other words, the non-listed entity which is party to the transaction takes over the listed company by virtue of acquiring more than 50% of the listed company's issued share capital and leaves the company's shareholders with less than 50% ownership. A reverse take-over is often referred to as a back door listing since the non-listed entity involved in the transaction will effectively become listed on the Exchange by acquiring shares of the listed company in exchange for assets, or through an amalgamation or merger, with the listed company.

The Exchange first introduced Listings Policy Statement No. 22 to regulate two significant problems with reverse take-overs. First, the Exchange had observed an inordinate length of time between the public disclosure of the take-over by a news release and the submission of the relevant documentation to the Exchange for approval. During this period, there was often a lack of substantive information, particularly of the affairs of the non- listed entity. Second, the Exchange was concerned that a reverse take-over may occur almost immediately following listing or completion of a public offering which brought into question the integrity of the disclosure documents filed in respect of the listing or offering.

The second problem was dealt with in a variety of ways. The current prohibition respecting reverse take-overs is to be found in Exchange Rule B.1.16, which prohibits a reverse take-over of a listed company until one year has elapsed from the initial full listing of the company's securities on the Exchange. There is no equivalent rule in the case of Exchange offerings under SMFs.

The first problem, essentially involving a gap in significant information for investors between the time the reverse take-over has been agreed to and announced by news release and its completion, has been resolved by having the listed company, as soon as an agreement in principle respecting the take-over occurs, seek a trading halt from the Exchange in its listed securities and then issue a news release describing the material particulars of the take-over. This trading halt, which may last upwards of six months, is maintained by the Exchange until the reverse take-over has been completed or terminated. However, if the Exchange is satisfied that substantial documentation is available to the Exchange (such as a draft filing statement, SMF or other similar disclosure document), and there appear to be no contentious filing issues raised, and satisfactory interim public disclosure in the format of a Form RTO (appendix to Listings Policy Statement No. 22), has been made, the Exchange will consider resuming trading in the listed company's securities prior to the actual closing of the transaction. It should be noted that the Exchange will only consider resuming trading in the listed securities of companies which have entered into transactions which, when closed, will result in the listed company greatly exceeding the Exchange's initial listing, financial and expenditure requirements. This discretion to resume trading is used only rarely, and then very cautiously.

The Form RTO, which under previous Policy Statements was a mandatory filing, is now, under the current Policy Statement, an optional filing to be made with the Exchange shortly after the trading halt has occurred. The Exchange may require that it be filed, and listed companies are encouraged to prepare and file the Form, as a means of giving investors and the Exchange interim disclosure. The Form RTO requires disclosure of the following information:

- the name of the listed company;
- particulars of the listed company, specifically, the original listing date, material share issuances in the last 30 days and the name of all corporate contact persons;
- the date of the agreement respecting the reverse take-over (including evidence of the listed company's directors' approval and a signed agreement);
- the particulars of the reverse take-over, specifically, the name of the unlisted entity and, if the unlisted entity is a company, (a) the names of its directors and senior officers including their municipality of residence, other positions they hold in the company and their principal occupations, (b) its corporate or executive offices, (c) a summary of its material assets and liabilities, (d) the holders of 10% or greater of the equity shares of the unlisted company, (e) a description of its business, (f) financial information, (g) management information, and (h) share capital structure;
- a description of the terms of the reverse take-over including proposed consideration, earn-out provisions and related share transactions;

- a description of the financial arrangements for the reverse take-over;
- a description of the resulting company's management, business, financial condition, promotional/marketing arrangements and remuneration schemes;
- a description of all shareholder, regulatory and other approvals required; and
- a description of closing requirements and risk factors.

The Form RTO must be certified accurate by a representative of the listed company, and should be filed along with the appropriate agreements, technical reports and valuations, opinions, directors' minutes and pro-forma financial statements. A Filing Statement, or SMF if an Exchange offering is required to finance the transaction, a new listing agreement and a letter signed by a Member stating that it has complied with the Exchange's Member sponsorship policy (see Chapter 3) must be filed with the Exchange in order to complete the filing requirements of the Exchange set out in Listings Policy Statement No. 22. This latter filing must usually be made within 60 days of the agreement in principle being entered.

Listings Policy Statement No. 22 implicitly requires that the company resulting from the reverse take-over must meet all of the Exchange's minimum initial listing requirements. The Exchange may require the securities of the listed company to be issued under the reverse take-over be fully or partially escrowed. The Exchange will also require the proposed new management to have the necessary knowledge or expertise to manage the business affairs of the resulting company and be otherwise acceptable to the Exchange and the Superintendent of Brokers.

The proposed reverse take-over must be approved by the shareholders of the listed company where the transaction involves the issuance by the listed company of 20% or more of its issued share capital or where the transaction otherwise results in a change in the effective control of the listed company. The information circular sent to shareholders should clearly state that the proposed transaction is subject to regulatory approval if this approval has not been obtained prior to the mailing of the information circular. In this regard, the Exchange recommends that its approval be obtained prior to the submission to the listed company's shareholders for their approval.

Where a financing is integral to successfully completing the reverse take-over, the Exchange may accept the pricing for a public financing or private placement based on the market price for the listed company's shares prior to public announcement of the reverse take-over.

Incentive stock options will generally not be accepted by the Exchange unless they have been granted at least 30 days after closing of the reverse take-over and resumption of trading.

CHAPTER FIVE

Exchange Approval Requirements

GENERAL

Following the listing of a company's shares on the Exchange, all of the company's business affairs become subject to review by the Exchange. Companies which are the least developed (categorized as Venture Companies) will receive the most scrutiny from the Exchange and as the company matures in its corporate development, the Exchange will regulate its activities to a lesser extent. Companies which attain the minimum requirements associated with the Exchange's senior category, the exempt status, receive the least scrutiny. The rationale for such scrutiny is that the Exchange allows for the listing of junior companies at a very early stage of development and, because of the minimum standards imposed on listing, the Exchange should, in the interests of shareholders and the investing public, monitor their development to the stage where they have demonstrated their viability and potential.

Not all activities of the listed company are subject to review by the Exchange. The listing agreement entered into between the Exchange and the company at the time of listing sets out the obligations of the company, including the circumstances in which filings must be made, notices must be given and approvals must be obtained. It is pursuant to the listing agreement that the Exchange obtains its regulatory jurisdiction over the company's affairs. In the case of SMFs, the Exchange also obtains jurisdiction under paragraph 58(1)(c) of the *Securities Act*. In furtherance of its ability to regulate, the Exchange has developed a number of rules and both written and unwritten policies (which are the subject of other Chapters) to establish parameters in which certain transactions may be conducted and to prescribe the filing requirements relating to such transactions. These transactions, regarded as material changes, require Exchange approval before they may be conducted or consummated. It should be noted that the word approval does not connote that the Exchange passes judgment on the merits of a particular company's transaction. Rather, the Exchange itself prefers listed companies to use the terminology Exchange acceptance rather than Exchange approval.

Notwithstanding the Exchange's preference, Exchange approval is used here since they are the words most commonly used to describe the Exchange regulatory process.

The following is a discussion of those transactions regarded as material changes, the methods by which prior Exchange approval may be sought and the general exemptions from prior Exchange approval which are afforded to each category of listed company where the material change is the acquisition or disposition of assets. The discussion will also deal with additional filing requirements which are imposed by the Exchange on listed companies, however, it will not deal with any filing requirements imposed by the *Act* and to which listed companies are subject.

PRIOR EXCHANGE APPROVAL

The most significant provision of a company's listing agreement with the Exchange provides that a company must give the Exchange prompt written notice of any proposed material change in its business, property or affairs. Such notice is to be given not later than 30 days from the proposed change, unless the Exchange's Rules or Listings Policy Statements provide otherwise, by filing with the Exchange a Filing Statement, SMF or any other documentation as the Exchange may permit or require. In addition, the company must not proceed with these changes until the Exchange has accepted for filing the documentation disclosing the material change. The company may, however, be exempted by the Exchange, either generally or specifically, from the requirements to give notice and to obtain prior acceptance of the change before proceeding.

It is often the case that the documentation respecting the material change cannot be prepared within 30 days from the proposed change. For example, in the case of an asset acquisition, the negotiation and preparation of formal agreements and the examination and report preparation by an engineer, geologist or consultant who must comment on the natural resource property or non-resource asset (as the case may be), may take considerably longer than 30 days to prepare. In such circumstances, every effort should be made to prepare the documentation as quickly as possible and to file it with the Exchange as soon as practicable. With respect to certain material changes, specific policies of the Exchange which regulate these changes may strictly impose a 30 day filing period. Failure to file within this period may result in the Exchange refusing to accept the transaction as filed (as discussed in other Chapters).

In response to late, incomplete or inadequate filings, the Exchange may take certain remedial action. As a measure against late filings, the Exchange may halt or suspend trading in the company's shares pending a satisfactory arrangement with respect to submission of documentation. This action is taken only in exceptional circumstances. To provide immediate interim disclosure of a material change, it may accept an initial submission of a filing as to form only, pending formal review. The documentation and any subsequent amendment could be made public provided the Exchange indicated on the face pages of the documentation that the disclosure had not been vetted for Exchange acceptance. Where late or inadequate responses to deficiencies are provided, the Exchange may withdraw the filing from further review, subject to giving prior notice of such withdrawal to the company.

In view of the requirement for prior approval to a proposed material change, a listed company announcing the material change by way of news release should include a statement that the proposed transaction is subject to regulatory approval. Likewise, any contract entered into by the listed company providing for the material change should be made subject to obtaining regulatory approval to the transaction. If a listed company proceeds to complete a transaction for which the required documentation has not been accepted or has been rejected for filing by the Exchange, the Exchange has the power to delist the company's securities from the Exchange.

MATERIAL CHANGE

The listing agreement for a non-exempt company enumerates the following as situations considered to constitute a material change in a listed company's business, property or assets. This list is not intended to be exhaustive:

- any agreement to issue shares or other securities;
- any stock option, share purchase warrant or stock purchase plan;
- any change in the board of directors or senior officers;
- any management contract and any non-arm's length transaction;
- any change of name, capital reorganization, merger or amalgamation;
- any acquisition of its own securities or of the securities of another company;
- any non-arm's length change in the beneficial ownership of the shares or other securities of the company which may materially affect control;
- any loan or advance of funds to another person or company that is not wholly owned;
- any change in the undertaking of the company;
- any mortgaging, hypothecating or charging in any way any of its assets; and

- any acquisition or disposition of assets involving costs or proceeds exceeding the amounts from time to time prescribed, either generally or specifically, by the Exchange.

The Exchange requires prompt written notice of and prior approval to these changes before they are proceeded with, unless the company is exempted from these requirements.

It should be noted that one of the above changes, namely, a change in the beneficial ownership of a listed company's securities which may materially affect control of the company, is limited to non-arm's length changes. An individual may acquire control of a listed company through share purchases in open market transactions which the company may not be aware of (even though ss.93 and 96 of the *Act* require disclosure of such acquisitions) and over which the company has no control. Accordingly, prior Exchange approval to such a change of control is not practical. Prior Exchange approval to a change of control is required where the change of control results from the issuance of a listed company's securities or from the transfer of a block of shares involving directors, officers, promoters or other insiders of the company. When a change of control requires an order under ss.33 and 59 of the Act to effect the transfer, the Superintendent of Brokers will not grant the order until the Exchange has approved the change of control. It should be noted that the rules respecting timely disclosure require disclosure of all changes in share ownership which materially affect control of a company, whether the changes are at arm's length or not (see Chapter 18).

The term material change for the purposes of securities regulation, is generally regarded as a change in the business, property, affairs or ownership of the company which would reasonably be expected to affect significantly the market price or the value of the company's securities. Thus, materiality is perceived from an investor's view point. In examining matters which constitute material changes for purposes of the listing agreement, it is evident that they may cover a vast number of transactions which could not be expected to have any affect on the market price of the listed company's securities. However, these changes are considered material by the Exchange for the purpose of monitoring the affairs of the junior company. In contrast, the listing agreement between the Exchange and an exempt company requires prior Exchange approval to very few transactions, which are discussed later in this Chapter.

Where the material change is reasonably expected to affect significantly the market price of the company's securities, the listed company may be required to file a *Securities Act* Form 27 with the Securities Commission as required by s.67 of the Act. A copy of the Form 27, which must be filed within ten days of the occurrence of the material change, should also be provided to the Exchange.

SMF

Where a material transaction is entered into at the time an Exchange offering is contemplated by a listed company, the transaction may be disclosed in an SMF, being the public offering document which qualifies the Exchange offering. Upon acceptance of the SMF by the Exchange, the transaction receives Exchange approval. If the proposed material change involves the acquisition of an asset which will require funding, either to make stipulated payments or to develop the asset, the Exchange will generally not approve the acquisition until it is satisfied that the company will have the financial means for this payment and development. If the company intends to finance the transaction by way of an Exchange offering, the transaction will not receive Exchange approval until the company has also obtained approval to the proposed Exchange offering by the acceptance of its SMF by the Exchange. In this situation, the proposed asset acquisition would be disclosed in the SMF and approved upon acceptance of the SMF.

The SMF is a prescribed form (Form 24) under the exemption found in paragraph 58(1)(c) of the *Act* and is very similar in content to a Filing Statement which is discussed in detail below. The material acquisition to be approved in the SMF is disclosed in Item 3, if it is a natural resource property, or in Item 4, if it is a non-resource asset. Reference is made to Item 1 of the Filing Statement for the nature of the disclosure regarding the acquisition of a natural resource property and a non-resource asset.

FILING STATEMENT

Where the material change does not occur at the time of an Exchange offering, the listed company must file a Filing Statement disclosing the material transaction unless the Exchange has exempted the company from the filing. The form of a Filing Statement is prescribed by the Exchange and, as mentioned above, is virtually identical in content to the SMF. The disclosure requirements are divided into nine items; the first item requires disclosure of the proposed material change. In general, the material change is to be described in sufficient detail to readily determine the nature of the change. Where applicable, the description must include the name and address of the parties to the material change agreement, the interest or benefit to be acquired by the company, the consideration paid or payable by the company for such interest or benefit and any applicable finder's fees. The form of Filing Statement sets out disclosure guidelines for the following six common material changes:

- the acquisition of a natural resource property;
- the acquisition of a non-resource asset;
- the acquisition of another company by purchase, take-over or amalgamation;
- a consolidation and name change;
- rights offerings and private placements; and
- the issuance or transfer of escrow shares.

Where material changes are described in Item 1 of the Filing Statement, they need not be fully described in any other items of the Filing Statement, but a reference to the Item 1 disclosure should be made under any applicable items.

With respect to the proposed acquisition of a natural resource property or a non-resource asset, the following general disclosure is required:

- the name and address of the vendor;
- the interest to be acquired by the company (and, in the case of a natural resource property, the company's contribution to costs and share in revenues (if not identical) and any applicable royalties, net smelter returns, carried interests, etc.);
- the total consideration paid or payable by the company (and, in the case of a natural resource property, any commitments respecting the property such as installments of cash or shares required to maintain options, exploration commitments or drilling obligations);
- if the property or asset was acquired by the vendor within one year of the company's acquisition, the cost of the property to the vendor;
- the name of any insider or promoter of the company who has held any interest in the property or asset during the past year; and
- details of any finder's fee to be paid by the company, including the name and address of the finder.

The specific disclosure respecting the proposed acquisition of a natural resource property should include the following:

- any material exploration or development work carried out on the property to date and the results, any exploration and development work which the company proposes to carry out and the planned expenditures from funds held by the company;
- if work on a mining property has established the existence of reserves of proven, probable or possible ore, the estimated tonnage and grade of each class of ore reserves as well as the name of the person making the estimates and the nature of that person's relationship to the company. If the property has no known ore reserves, this must be disclosed; and

- if reserves for an oil and gas property have been assigned in an acceptable engineering report, the report identified by author and date, the category, type and values assigned on a net cash flow basis using discount rates of 0% and the current industry rate for the evaluations. If the property has no known reserves of oil and gas, this must be disclosed.

In the case of the proposed acquisition of a non-resource asset, the following information should be described briefly:

- the business carried on or intended to be carried on by the company and the general development of this business within the past three years;
- the principal products or services, if the company's proposed business consists of the production or distribution of various products or the rendering of various services; and
- the location and general character of any material properties to be acquired, including buildings and plants, the nature of the title if the properties are not freehold properties and any material encumbrances to which the properties are subject.

The listed company's proposed acquisition of another company by purchase, take-over or amalgamation should include disclosure of the total purchase price to be paid, the take-over terms or amalgamation basis to acquire the other company (including any closing conditions, future consideration or contingencies) and a description of the assets of the company to be acquired and of any liabilities, commitments and undertakings assumed. Disclosure should also be made if an insider or promoter of the company is also an insider or promoter of the company to be acquired.

The disclosure respecting a proposed share consolidation and name change of the listed company should include the ratio on which the company's share capital will be consolidated and any other modifications to the company's share capital, the date of the shareholders' meeting approving the consolidation and name change and the date these changes are to be effected. All share capital disclosures appearing elsewhere in the Filing Statement should be described on a consolidated basis.

The material facts relating to a proposed rights offering of the listed company as outlined in Exchange Rule B.3.00, Part F. (described in Chapter 7), and the material facts relating to a proposed private placement of the listed company's securities as outlined in Listings Policy Statements Nos. 11 and 21 (described in Chapter 8) should be disclosed in Item 1 of the Filing Statement.

The proposed issuance of any escrow shares by the listed company will involve disclosure of the number of shares to be issued, the name and address of each recipient and their relationship to the company, the consideration paid or payable and the nature of any additional consideration to be paid (such as cash). If an asset is being acquired for the escrow shares, the asset should be described. In the case of the proposed transfer of escrow shares of the listed company, the disclosure should include the number of escrow shares to be sold by each transferor and the number of such shares to be purchased by each transferee as well as the name and address of each transferee, their relationship to the company and the consideration paid or payable. If a shareholders' meeting is required to approve the issuance or transfer of escrow shares, the date of the shareholders' meeting should also be disclosed.

The remaining eight items of the Filing Statement and the respective disclosure required by each item are outlined below.

Item 2 relates to the disclosure of financial information. The listed company's working capital as of a date within two months preceding the date of the Filing Statement must be disclosed and, if the company has investments in other entities, an itemized statement showing cost or book value and present market value of the investments must also be disclosed.

Item 3 contains the disclosures of material natural resource properties. A material natural resource property is defined as: *(a)* a property which is currently producing or being explored, *(b)* a property upon which exploration is planned within the next year, *(c)* a property which contains undiscounted reserves of oil and gas in excess of $50,000.00, or *(d)* a property upon which the company's acquisition and exploration costs to date exceed $100,000.00. For each material resource property, disclosure similar to that required in Item 1 of the Filing Statement must be made, where applicable. As well, for each property which is currently producing revenue for the listed company, the total revenue, net to the company, in the latest completed fiscal year and currently (on a monthly basis) must be provided.

Item 4 requires the disclosure of non-resource assets. For each material non-resource asset, disclosure similar to that required by Item 1 of the Filing Statement must be made.

Item 5 relates to the disclosure of certain corporate information. The authorized and issued share capital of the listed company must be disclosed together with a brief outline of any material rights and restrictions attached to the share capital such as voting, preference, conversion or redemption rights.

Item 6 contains disclosure relating to directors, officers, promoters and persons holding more than 10% of the equity shares of the company. The following information must be provided for each director, officer and promoter of the listed company:

- the full name and residential or postal address;
- all positions held with the company (for example, president, director or promoter);
- the number of equity shares of the company beneficially owned, directly or indirectly, separated by type into *(a)* escrow, *(b)* pooled, and *(c)* all other shares;
- the name of each current employer as well as the chief occupations in the previous five years: occupational descriptions should describe the functions actually performed;
- if any director, officer or promoter of the company is or has been within the past three years, a director, officer or promoter of any other reporting company *(a)* the number of the companies of which he is currently a director, officer or promoter, with indication that a list of the names of the companies will be available for inspection and *(b)* the name of any company which was, during the period he was a director, officer or promoter, struck off the Register of Companies by the Registrar of Companies, or other similar authority, or whose securities were the subject of a cease trade or suspension order for a period of more than 30 consecutive days together with the reasons for the striking, cease trade or suspension order;
- particulars of any director, officer, promoter or insider of the company receiving direct or indirect remuneration from the company within the past year, including the name of the recipient, the level of remuneration and the duties performed; and
- particulars of any director, officer, promoter or insider of the company receiving anything of value from the company within the past year, unless disclosed elsewhere in the Filing Statement. (Anything of value includes money, securities, property, contracts, options or rights of any kind, whether received directly or indirectly).

Disclosure must also be provided of the full name, residential or postal address and number of equity shares, separated by type into *(a)* escrow, *(b)* pooled, and *(c)* all other shares, beneficially owned by each person who is known by the company's directors to own beneficially, directly or indirectly, more than 10% of the equity shares of the company (other than directors, officers and promoters).

Item 7 contains the disclosure of options to purchase the company's securities. Disclosure must be made of all options, share purchase warrants, rights or agreements to issue securities by the listed company or by a present security holder, which have not been disclosed elsewhere in the Filing Statement. It should be noted that it is not only options in respect of the company's treasury shares which are required to be disclosed. This particular disclosure requirement is designed to compel disclosure of material option agreements entered into by any of the company's shareholders which the signatories to the Filing Statement are aware of or of which they should be aware.

Item 8 relates to the disclosure of the company's securities held in escrow, in pool or subject to hold restrictions. A brief description must be made of (a) the number and the material terms governing release and cancellation of all escrow shares, (b) the number and the material terms governing release of all pooled shares, and (c) the number and the material terms governing any other securities which are subject to an unexpired hold period originally imposed by the Exchange or the Superintendent of Brokers.

Item 9 entails the disclosure of any other material facts. Brief particulars of any other material facts not disclosed elsewhere in the Filing Statement are to be disclosed as well as (a) any actual or pending material legal proceedings to which the listed company is or is likely to be a party or of which any of its property is or is likely to be the subject, (b) any properties proposed to be acquired, or other transactions, for which regulatory approval is not being sought under the Filing Statement, and (c) any bonds, debentures, notes or other debt obligations outstanding. Additionally, reference must be made as to the place and a reasonable time at which the list of names of the reporting companies referred to in Item 6 may be inspected during the 30 day period after the Exchange publishes its Notice regarding acceptance of the Filing Statement.

The Filing Statement must be signed by two directors of the listed company who certify that the Filing Statement, together with the financial information and other reports where required, constitutes full, true and plain disclosure of all material facts in respect of the company's affairs.

For the purpose of preparing the Filing Statement, the form of Filing Statement defines company to include any subsidiary, year to mean a period of twelve months preceding the certificate date of the Filing Statement, associate, insider and promoter to have the same meaning as in s.1(1) of the *Act* and material to mean a fact or change that could reasonably be expected to have a significant effect on the market value of the company's securities (unless otherwise defined). Additionally, where the answer to any item refers to a company other than the listed company, the name of any insider or promoter of the listed company, who is also an insider, promoter or an associate of an insider of the other company, must be disclosed.

The Filing Statement is submitted to the Exchange together with the appropriate filing fee and the Exchange's fee for printing the Filing Statement. All material agreements, technical reports and other documents referred to in the Filing Statement also must be submitted in support of the Filing Statement. All technical reports must comply with the requirements of Securities Commission Local Policy Statements Nos. 3-01 and 3-04 (February 1, 1987), Forms 54 and 55 prescribed under the Act, National

Policy Statement No. 2A (April 22, 1983 as amended December 9, 1983) and National Policy Statement No. 2B (November 26, 1982). Following a review of the Filing Statement and supporting documentation by the Exchange, any comments of the Exchange are generally communicated in writing to the filing solicitor. When all comments have been dealt with to the satisfaction of the Exchange, the Filing Statement will be accepted for filing by the Exchange and will be printed by the Exchange for dissemination to its subscribers.

Where the material change involves the issuance of the listed company's securities, the Exchange will require confirmation that the securities will be issued in compliance with the *Act*. The applicable provision of the *Securities Act* which allows such issuance must be identified as well as the filing of any documents required for reliance on the provision. Where a ruling is required under ss.33 and 59 of the *Act* prior to such issuance, the Superintendent of Brokers will generally not make this ruling until the Exchange has accepted the Filing Statement for filing.

Material changes which occur after acceptance of the Filing Statement may be disclosed by way of an amendment to the Filing Statement (referred to as an Amended Filing Statement), provided any amendment is filed within six months of the date of the certificate to the Filing Statement.

It should be noted that a provision of the listing agreement between a listed company and the Exchange requires that Filing Statements and any amended Filing Statements also must be filed with the Superintendent of Brokers at the same time they are filed with the Exchange.

FORMAL LETTERS

The listing agreement between an exempt company and the Exchange does not require the exempt company to give notice in a Filing Statement of proposed material changes in its business, property or affairs. Such changes are disclosed to the Exchange in a formal letter which must set out the important particulars of the proposed changes.

There are also certain types of material changes for which the Exchange does not generally require a Filing Statement from non-exempt companies. The granting of incentive stock options, changes in directors or senior officers and management contracts are examples of material changes which are usual and recurring and are generally submitted to the Exchange for acceptance in a formal letter. Where the information required by a Filing Statement is provided in other materials circulated to the listed company's shareholders, such as a rights offering circular for a rights offering, the Exchange waives the requirement for a Filing Statement and Exchange approval to the material transaction may be sought in a formal letter.

The requirement for a Filing Statement from a non-exempt company is determined by the Exchange on a case-by-case basis. Where there is uncertainty of both the filing requirements and the acceptability of the proposed terms of a material change, a formal letter describing the change should be filed with the Exchange as early as possible to obtain acceptance in principle to the terms and clarification of the filing requirements. It should be noted that no proposed material change will be approved by the Exchange under an SMF, Filing Statement or otherwise, if the listed company is delinquent with other filings, statutory or otherwise, required by the Exchange and the Superintendent of Brokers.

GENERAL EXEMPTIONS

A. General

One of the material changes enumerated in the Exchange's listing agreement with non-exempt companies is the purchase or sale of assets involving costs or proceeds exceeding amounts prescribed by the Exchange. The acquisition or disposition which has associated with it costs or proceeds below the prescribed amounts is exempt from the requirement to obtain Exchange approval before it is completed. The prescribed amounts are set forth in Exchange Listings Policy Statement No. 9 and have been increased by the Exchange from time to time.

There are certain limitations, however, on the availability of these exemptions. First, by virtue of the express terms of Listings Policy Statement No. 9, they relate only to transactions at arm's length with insiders of the listed company, as that term is defined in s.1(1) of the *Act*. Second, the source of funds utilized for the purchase of assets must be unallocated working capital; the funds must not have been designated in a previous disclosure document for another specified purpose. Third, the listed company must be up-to-date in its filings, statutory or otherwise, with the Exchange and under the *Act*. Fourth, the company's shares must be posted for trading, that is, not suspended from trading, on the Exchange.

Specific reference should be made to two applications of these general exemptions. Where the acquisition of a natural resource property is by an option agreement which requires periodic option payments and share issuances as well as staged expenditure commitments on the property, the Exchange takes the view that all such payments, share issuances and commitments form the acquisition costs. Accordingly, they should be added in the aggregate to determine the total acquisition costs.

The other application relates to the advance of funds by a listed company toward the acquisition of an asset. A company should not advance funds for a particular transaction up to the prescribed amounts without prior Exchange approval, where the total acquisition costs exceed the prescribed amounts. Exchange approval to the acquisition should be sought prior to the time the listed company is required to pay any funds.

Although those transactions which fit within the general exemptions do not require the approval of the Exchange before being completed, they do remain subject to the timely disclosure requirements of the Exchange, as set forth in Exchange Listings Policy Statement No. 10 and to the timely disclosure provisions contained in s.67 of the *Act*. As well, the relevant documentation must be submitted to the Exchange together with the appropriate filing fee subsequent to the transaction.

B. Venture Company

In the case of a Venture Company, a transaction or a series of related transactions involving an acquisition or disposition of assets at arm's length to insiders of the Venture Company is not subject to prior Exchange approval where the total acquisition costs or disposition proceeds, including cash and securities, do not exceed $300,000.00 so long as no more than 100,000 shares of the Venture Company are being issued as part of the transaction. This exemption is limited to asset transactions and excludes any transaction that falls within any other Listings Policy Statement including Listings Policy Statements No. 3, 4, 6 and 8.

C. Resource or Commercial/Industrial Company

Arm's length asset transactions conducted by a Resource or Commercial/Industrial Company have the same filing exemption available to them as applies to a Venture Company as discussed above. However, any arm's length transaction in an amount which exceeds $300,000.00 in value, which may include the value of no more than 100,000 shares, may be filed utilizing a simplified and expedited filing procedure provided for in Listings Policy Statement No. 9. A notice is to be filed describing the proposed material change and enclosing all pertinent documents (in draft or final executed form) as they exist at the time of the notice. The notice also is to propose the completed documents, including technical reports, which will be filed with the Exchange to obtain final acceptance of the material change and the time when the documents will be filed, which should not be later than 30 days from the date of the notice.

The Exchange will advise within ten business days if the notice is acceptable for filing in principle and may add to, or delete from, the list of proposed final documents disclosed in the notice for filing to obtain final acceptance. If no response is received from the Exchange within ten business days, then the notice of material change is considered accepted in principle and the final documents for obtaining final acceptance as proposed are acceptable. The transaction may proceed on acceptance of the notice in principle, however, the company is at risk if it fails to file final documentation within the suggested time period as acceptance may be withdrawn.

If a notice is not accepted for filing, the Exchange will have up to an additional five business days from the date of the refusal to provide the requirements to obtain its acceptance or to provide the reason for refusal of the notice.

Notice of a non-arm's length transaction by a Resource or Commercial/ Industrial Company can be filed in the same manner as discussed above, however, the transaction cannot proceed until final acceptance is provided by the Exchange (following the filing, review and acceptance of the final completed documents).

In addition to the expedited and simplified filing procedure available to Resource or Commercial/Industrial Companies in respect of asset transactions, these companies are also provided special treatment under certain policy statements of the Exchange, specifically, Listings Policy Statements Nos. 1, 3, 4, 6, 7 and 8 as discussed more specifically in Chapters 9, 11, 12, 13 and 15.

D. Exempt Company

The requirements to obtain exempt status have been described in Chapter 3 and relate to the most advanced type of company listed on the Exchange. An exempt company's transactions involving an arm's length acquisition or disposition of assets do not require prior Exchange approval. The listing agreement between the Exchange and an exempt company specifies that only the following agreements or changes require Exchange approval before proceeding:

- any agreement to issue shares or other securities;
- any stock option agreement or stock purchase plan; and
- any change of name, capital reorganization, merger or amalgamation.

In Listings Policy Statement No. 9, the Exchange has further narrowed the requirement for prior Exchange acceptance for an exempt company to those transactions involving the following:

- the proposed issuance of shares or other securities to persons not at arm's length to insiders of the company that would give rise to the filing of a material change report in the company's reporting jurisdiction;
- proposed incentive stock options or stock option plans which exceed

the Exchange's incentive stock option parameters established for Resource or Commercial/Industrial Companies; and
• any proposed change of name and/or capital reorganization.

As is the case with all these exemptions from prior Exchange approval, the exempt company status does not affect the company's responsibility to comply with the Exchange's timely disclosure policy, and the timely disclosure provisions found in s.67 of the Act, or from the obligation to submit all documentation relevant to the company's transactions with the Exchange together with the appropriate filing fees, all of which are prescribed by Listings Policy Statement No. 9.

QUARTERLY REPORTS

The *Regulation to the Securities Act* requires that a company listed only on the Exchange must file a Quarterly Report with the Securities Commission and the Exchange in the form prescribed under the *Act*. It must do so for each quarter of its fiscal year. The Quarterly Report is made public by both the Exchange and the Commission.

The first Quarterly Report to be filed by a company after it has obtained a receipt for its prospectus from the Superintendent of Brokers must cover the period from the date of the receipt to the end of the quarter within the company's fiscal year. The first Report, however, must not cover a period shorter than two months nor longer than five months and each succeeding Quarterly Report must cover a three month period. The Reports are required to be filed within 60 days of the end of each fiscal quarter.

The Quarterly Report provides certain specified information for each fiscal quarter including the following:

• financial statements, in accordance with s.135(4) to 135(6) of the *Regulation to the Securities Act* as well as a summary balance sheet;
• for the current year up to date, a breakdown of expenditures and costs which are included in deferred costs, exploration and development expenses, cost of sales or general and administrative expenses, including aggregate amounts paid to related parties;
• for the quarter under review, a summary of securities issued and options granted;
• as at the end of the quarter, full particulars of the authorized and issued share capital, outstanding options, convertible securities and securities held in escrow or pool and a list of directors;
• brief details of any significant event or transaction which occurred during the period.

Failure to file a Quarterly Report within the required time period will result in the company being added to the Superintendent of Brokers' defaulting issuer list and may result in the Superintendent issuing an order under s.144 of the *Act* that all trading in the company's securities cease. Such an order is not revoked until the company furnishes the required Quarterly Report. Contemporaneously with the cease trade order, the Exchange will suspend trading in the company's securities.

MONTHLY STATEMENTS OF SOURCE AND APPLICATION OF FUNDS

Where a listed company has conducted an Exchange offering, the Exchange letter accepting the SMF qualifying the Exchange offering will, in most cases, require the listed company to provide the Exchange with a monthly statement of source and application of funds, signed by two directors of the company. The first Statement must cover the month in which the Exchange offering was conducted. Thereafter, the Statements must be filed for each calendar month until all of the proceeds from the Exchange offering have been expended.

While the monthly statements of source and application of funds are not available for public inspection, they are reviewed by Exchange officials to monitor the manner in which the proceeds from the Exchange offering are being utilized in relation to the use of proceeds disclosure provided in the SMF. If the company fails to file the statements of source and application of funds, the Exchange may halt or suspend trading in the company's securities until the statements are filed and an explanation given for the non-compliance.

The statements of source and application of funds are not required to be filed by an exempt company and are generally required from a Resource or Commercial/Industrial Company. They must be filed by a Venture Company.

CHAPTER SIX

Exchange Offerings By Listed Companies

GENERAL

Once a company's securities are listed on the Exchange, public financings may be conducted through the facilities of the Exchange; these financings are commonly called Exchange offerings and they are conducted pursuant to a public disclosure document called an SMF. The Exchange offering is the most common method by which junior listed companies raise public equity capital. Following the sale of the company's securities pursuant to the SMF, the securities may be traded immediately on the Exchange. No application is required to have the securities posted and called for trading on the Exchange.

The *Securities Act* exempts an Exchange offering from Part 7 of the *Act*, the prospectus qualification provisions, by virtue of an exemption contained in paragraph 58(1)(c) of the *Act* which requires that the SMF be filed with and accepted by both the Superintendent of Brokers and the Exchange. The SMF contains similar but less extensive disclosure than that contained in a prospectus. Although the SMF is filed with the Superintendent, it is primarily reviewed by the Exchange. Because of this review process and the less onerous disclosure in the SMF, an Exchange offering generally receives regulatory approval in a shorter period of time than the initial distribution (described in Chapter 4).

The following discussion deals with junior listed companies conducting Exchange offerings in British Columbia only. The content of the SMF and the approval process for Exchange offerings will be discussed in this Chapter as will the different types of Exchange offerings which may be conducted and the compensation which may be given to an underwriter or an agent for participating in the Offerings.

SMF

Every purchaser of securities in an Exchange offering is entitled to receive an SMF in connection with a purchase. S.121 of the *Regulation to the*

Securities Act requires that an SMF, like a prospectus, contain full, true and plain disclosure of all material facts relating to the securities being sold. If there are materially false or misleading statements in the SMF, the purchaser may, under certain circumstances, initiate an action to rescind the purchase.

The form of SMF is prescribed as Form 24 under the Act. Unlike the prospectus, there is no requirement for a preliminary SMF and, accordingly, an SMF must be filed in final form. An SMF may, however, require updating prior to its acceptance in response to deficiencies or as a result of changes during the period between filing and acceptance. As with a prospectus, if a material change occurs after an SMF has been accepted and before completion of the distribution under it, the listed company must file an amendment to the SMF no later than ten days after the change occurs. There is no prescribed form for an amendment.

The format and disclosure requirements of an SMF are very similar to those of a Filing Statement (discussed in detail in Chapter 5) with three exceptions. The first major difference is in Item 1. Item 1 of the SMF requires disclosure of the plan of distribution whereas Item 1 of the Filing Statement requires disclosure of the material change for which the Filing Statement is submitted. The plan of distribution section must disclose the following:

- the manner in which the securities being offered are to be distributed, including the particulars of any underwriting or sub-underwriting agreements or option or sub-option agreements which are outstanding or proposed or any assignments of such agreements and any rights of first refusal on future offerings;
- the particulars of any payments in cash or securities or other consideration made or to be made to a promoter, finder or any other person in connection with the offering;
- the name and address of any market maker (ie: a person or company who buys and sells the company's securities on a continuous basis with a view to creating and/or maintaining an orderly market for the company's securities) and the approximate number of the company's securities under the market maker's control;
- the number of the company's securities beneficially owned, directly or indirectly, by the underwriter or agent;
- if any securities are being sold pursuant to the SMF by a shareholder of the company, the name, address and number of securities beneficially owned by the shareholder, directly or indirectly, the number being offered and the number to be owned after the offering. A statement must be made that the securities of the shareholder will not be sold until the distribution of the company's securities has been completed.

The second major difference between an SMF and a Filing Statement is in Item 2. The Filing Statement requires disclosure of the company's working capital and investments in securities whereas Item 2 of the SMF requires disclosure of how the proceeds from the Exchange offering are to be spent (referred to as the "use of proceeds"). The disclosure must include the following:

- the principal purposes, in tabular form, for which the net proceeds and any material amounts of working capital on hand will be used and the estimated amount to be spent on each;
- in the case of a best efforts offering, a statement regarding priority usage of the actual proceeds where the entire offering may not be sold;
- in the event that proceeds from the offering will be insufficient to rectify any material working capital deficiency, an explanation as to how such working capital deficiency will be rectified so as to render the company solvent upon completion of the offering; and
- particulars of any provisions or arrangements made for holding any part of the net proceeds in trust or subject to the fulfillment of any conditions (such as receipt of a minimum subscription).

The use of proceeds section is one of the most critical disclosure items in the SMF. The listed company must ensure that the proceeds from the Exchange offering are expended in the manner set out and any redirection of the proceeds would require prior Exchange approval. Such approval would generally be granted where there is valid justification for redirecting the funds.

Items 3 to 9 of the SMF are virtually identical to the corresponding items in the Filing Statement except that certain information concerning material natural resource properties must be provided in tabular form in Item 3 of the SMF. The last major difference between the SMF and the Filing Statement is the requirement to include in the SMF (as is the case with a prospectus) certain financial statements and technical reports.

The requirements for financial statements to be included in the SMF are provided in Item 10 of the SMF. The SMF must include financial statements for the latest financial year and for any part of a subsequent financial year up to a date not more than 60 days before the date of submission of the SMF. Where the financial statements are prepared for part of a financial year, comparative figures for the comparable period in the prior year are not required. The interim financial statements may be prepared by management or by a public accountant who must give an auditor's communication suggested for these circumstances by the Handbook of the Canadian Institute of Chartered Accountants. All financial statements included in the SMF must be approved by the company's directors and the approval must be evidenced by the signatures on the balance sheet of two directors, duly authorized to signify such approval.

The financial statements must contain a balance sheet, a statement of surplus or deficit and a statement of changes in financial position. In addition, the financial statements of an industrial company still in the process of developing its production capacity or a natural resource company not yet in production must also include an analysis of deferred charges. An industrial company with an acceptable sales base or a natural resource company in production must also provide a statement of income.

The technical reports to be included in the SMF depend on how the proceeds from the Exchange offering are to be spent. Where a company engaged in the exploration and development of natural resources is allocating funds for exploration or development, an engineering report prepared by a qualified and independent engineer or geologist must be filed with the SMF. As is required in the case of a prospectus, the report must be prepared in accordance with Forms 54 and 55, prescribed under the *Act*, National Policy Statement No. 2A (April 22, 1983 as amended December 9, 1983), National Policy Statement No. 2B (November 26, 1982) and Securities Commission Local Policy Statement No. 3-01 (February 1, 1987). The report must describe such matters as the location of the property, the geological environment, prior exploration and development work, recommended exploration and development programs and the costs of the recommended programs. The program costs must correspond to the amounts allocated in the use of proceeds section of the SMF.

Where a company is acquiring or developing a non-resource asset on which proceeds from the Exchange offering are to be spent, a technical report which complies with Securities Commission Local Policy Statement No. 3-04 (February 1, 1987) must be filed with the SMF (as with a prospectus). While the technical report may be prepared by management, it must be reviewed and commented on by a qualified and independent consultant. The technical report must include such matters as a description of the project and implementation schedule for the project, details of the project management team, an evaluation and assessment of the product, service or technology, potential competition, any proprietary protection and the marketing and financial plans. While the engineering report or a summary of the report must be printed in the SMF of a natural resource company, the technical report for a non-resource company is not required to be printed in the SMF. However, the SMF must state the location where the technical report is available for review.

The SMF, which will be comprised of the nine items of disclosure, financial statements and technical report (if required) must be signed by the listed company's chief executive officer, chief financial officer and two directors, all who must certify that the SMF constitutes full, true and plain disclosure of all material facts relating to the securities to be offered by the SMF. As well, an underwriter or agent involved in the Exchange offering must certify that, to the best of its knowledge, information and belief, the SMF constitutes full, true and plain disclosure of all material facts relating to the securities to be offered by the SMF. All signatures are contained on the final page of the SMF which is referred to as the "certificate page".

In a decision of the Securities Commission, *In the Matter of Banco Resources Ltd.* (December 17, 1987), the Commission found that an SMF of Banco Resources Ltd. (Banco) pursuant to which an Exchange offering had been conducted, did not constitute full, true and plain disclosure at the time it was certified by Banco's directors and that, following the certification, the SMF became totally misleading when the Exchange offering became largely an issuance of shares to Banco's president in settlement of debt rather than the sale of shares for the purposes set out in the use of proceeds section of the SMF. The Commission found that Banco's directors failed to conduct the due diligence necessary to meet the statutory obligation to provide full, true and plain disclosure of all material facts relating to Banco and that it was in the public interest for the directors to incur some penalty. In penalizing the directors, the Commission ordered that the availability of certain trading exemptions set out in the *Act* be denied to the directors for periods ranging from two years to twenty years. The Commission further commented that it was not acceptable for a listed company, its directors and underwriters to rely on the Exchange and the Superintendent of Brokers in lieu of the directors and underwriters conducting a due diligence review and that those participating in British Columbia's securities market should regard the Commission's decision as notice that it will apply the provisions of the *Securities Act* firmly, where it determines that there has been behavior prejudicial to the public interest.

THE APPROVAL PROCESS

As mentioned above, the Exchange has primary responsibility for ensuring that the listed company's SMF complies with the legal and regulatory policy requirements of the Superintendent of Brokers and the Exchange. The Exchange is principally concerned with the proposed corporate transactions, particularly share issuances and the use of proceeds, and whether the Exchange offering complies with Exchange Rules. The Superintendent's primary review function relates to ensuring compliance with statutory requirements such as the filing of insider reports by the directors and senior officers, the filing of Quarterly Reports in the prescribed form and the filing and mailing to shareholders of required financial statements. The Superintendent is also concerned with whether the individuals who manage and conduct the business affairs of the listed company are acceptable. These vetting procedures of the Superintendent and the Exchange were implemented to expedite the review and approval process of the SMF.

The process involved in obtaining acceptance of the SMF by the Superintendent and the Exchange and in subsequently completing the Exchange offering, commences with preparation of the SMF and supporting documentation. The additional documents to be submitted with the SMF are itemized in Securities Commission Local Policy Statement No. 3-26 (February 1, 1987). The Superintendent must receive, along with the prescribed filing fee, the following documents:

- the SMF;
- a statement (signed by a director or secretary of the company) confirming the names of the individuals who comprise the company's audit committee, that the company has mailed to shareholders all mailings required by the *Company Act* and that Quarterly Report filings (for exchange issuers) are up-to-date;
- a Form 4 (prescribed under the *Act*) for any director, senior officer or market maker (other than the underwriters or agents), who has not submitted a Form 4 within the preceding three years;
- statements signed by the directors and senior officers confirming that their Form 4's have been submitted (if applicable) and that their insider reports are up-to-date;
- any applications for required rulings under the *Act* covering the issuance of the company's shares (pursuant to transactions to be approved by the Exchange in the SMF); and
- where an acquisition disclosed in the SMF involves a material share issuance (ie: 20% or more of the company's issued shares), an evaluation or technical report which supports the value of the assets being acquired for the company's shares.

The supporting documentation to be filed with the Exchange, together with the appropriate filing fee, is as follows:

- the SMF;
- the same statement that is filed with the Superintendent of Brokers respecting required mailings to shareholders and Quarterly Report filings;
- the required financial statements, including certified copies of the directors' resolutions approving same;
- an executed underwriting agreement or agency agreement;
- the required technical report and the written consent of the author to the inclusion of the report in the SMF;

76

- title opinions of mining properties being acquired or on which proceeds from the Exchange offering are intended to be spent; and
- certified copies of all material contracts not previously filed with the Exchange.

The filings are reviewed by the regulatory bodies and any comments and deficiencies of the Superintendent of Brokers and the Exchange are provided to the filing solicitor for the listed company and, in certain circumstances, to the listed company and its underwriter or agent. All responses to the deficiencies must be provided to both the Superintendent and the Exchange. The responses are then reviewed by the Superintendent and the Exchange and when all deficiencies have been dealt with to their satisfaction, the SMF will be accepted. The acceptance date of the SMF is referred to as the effective date, which will be at least two days following clearance of the deficiencies. The two days are required for the Exchange to issue an Exchange Notice advising of the proposed Exchange offering and for the company to print and deliver the SMF.

The listed company must deliver to the Exchange at least 50 copies of the SMF no later than 12:00 noon on the trading day immediately preceding its effective date, and at least 240 copies of the SMF not later than 9:00 a.m. on its effective date. The number of copies may vary depending on the Exchange's needs. An Exchange offering must be completed within 180 calendar days of the effective date, except in the case of underwritten Exchange offerings, which have no requirements limiting the length of time for the offering.

GENERAL RULES

Parts A to E of Exchange Rule B.3.00 deal with Exchange offerings and the types of Exchange offerings which may be conducted, namely, the underwriting, the best efforts agency offering, the fixed price agency offering of shares and the fixed price agency offering of units. Exchange Rule C.1.28 to C.1.34 regulates how Exchange offerings are to be conducted on the trading floor of the Exchange. Unless otherwise indicated, the remainder of this Chapter is a discussion of the provisions of Rules B.3.00 and C.1.00.

All listed companies are required to effect their public offerings, whether to the public in British Columbia or otherwise, through the facilities of the Exchange. There are two exceptions to this requirement, one being where the estimated gross proceeds of the offering (exclusive of proceeds from the exercise of options or warrants) exceeds $10,000,000.00. The second exception is where the securities of the company are inter-listed on a recognized stock exchange, the proposed offering is to be made in compliance with the rules of that stock exchange and either *(a)* the company is an exempt company or a Resource or Commercial/Industrial Company, or *(b)* the company is not an exempt company or a Resource or Commercial/Industrial Company provided that the portion of the offering, if any, to be sold in British Columbia is effected through the facilities of the Exchange.

An underwriter or an agent must not assign any underwriting, option or agency agreement or any rights thereunder, nor enter into any sub-underwriting, sub-option or sub-agency agreement unless the Exchange has given its prior approval. This does not restrict the right of an underwriter or an agent to offer selling group participation in the normal course of the brokerage business to selling groups of other licensed dealers, brokers and investment dealers provided disclosure is made in the SMF.

An underwriter or an agent of either a best efforts offering or fixed price agency offering, who wishes to put-through all or a part of the underwriting or offering at one price, must offer at the same price not less than 20% of the first 500,000 securities, not less than 10% of the next 500,000 securities and not less than 5% of the balance available for put-through to other Members of the Exchange as provided in Exchange Rule C.1.28. A put-through means the same Member has an order to buy and an order to sell a security at the same price. The agent under a best efforts offering also has available another method to effect a put-through which is provided in Exchange Rule C.1.32. Securities acquired pursuant to the exercise of a greenshoe option (described later in this Chapter) are included in determining the number of securities to be offered to other Members of the Exchange.

During the period in which the Exchange offering is being conducted and for a period of 30 trading days after the offering, an underwriter or an agent may buy and sell the listed company's securities in the open market for the purpose of maintaining an orderly market of the company's securities.

In accordance with Exchange Rules C.1.33 and C.1.34, an underwriter or an agent must prepare a list showing, to the best of its knowledge and belief, the names and addresses of the beneficial purchasers of the securities sold in the Exchange offering together with the respective number of securities purchased, the date upon which each purchase took place and the price paid per security. Each list must be filed with the Exchange within five business days of completion of the Exchange offering.

Following completion of an Exchange offering, the listed company must have a minimum number of shares held by a minimum number of beneficial shareholders, exclusive of insiders (as that term is defined in s.1(1) of the *Act*), each holding one or more board lots. Specifically, a Venture Company must have at least 200 shareholders holding not less than 300,000 shares in the aggregate, a Resource or Commercial/Industrial

Company must have at least 250 shareholders holding not less than 300,000 shares in the aggregate and an exempt company must have at least 300 shareholders holding not less than 350,000 shares in the aggregate. The Exchange is considering imposing the requirements of a Resource or Commercial/Industrial Company to a Venture Company.

The total net proceeds from an Exchange offering must be at least $50,000.00 and the net price per share of shares sold in the Exchange offering must not be less than $0.15, with one exception: where a listed company undergoes a capital reorganization involving a consolidation of its share capital within three months prior to the date of an SMF, the minimum net price per share of the Exchange offering pursuant to the SMF must be the greater of $0.15 or $0.07 multiplied by the consolidation ratio.

An underwriting, fixed price agency offering and best efforts agency offering, through an Exchange offering, have minimum requirements imposed by Exchange Rule B.3.00, discussed below. Under Exchange Rule B.3.00, an Exchange offering by way of underwriting or best efforts offering can only be made of shares and not units. Accordingly, a fixed price agency offering must be used where the listed company is proposing to sell units. A Venture Company is not permitted to undertake a unit offering until its shares have been listed for a period of time considered sufficient by the Exchange to establish an orderly market.

UNDERWRITINGS

A. The Distribution

In an underwriting of a listed company's shares, the total number of shares which may be underwritten at any one price is at the discretion of the Exchange, and will be subject to the financial requirements of the listed company. The net price per share to the company may be at a discount as negotiated between the listed company and the underwriter. However, the minimum net price to the company must be $0.15 per share.

In an underwriting, the underwriter purchases the listed company's shares on the effective date of the SMF. The underwriter is not restricted to a minimum period of time in which to conduct the Exchange offering. This is not a consequence of a particular Exchange Rule but is, rather, a consequence of the omission of the *Act* to include an SMF in the lapse provisions contained in s.122 of the *Regulation to the Securities Act* and in s.51 of the *Act*. However, as a matter of practice, the offering is usually conducted by the underwriter on the trading day, or next few trading days, following the effective date by crossing the shares on the trading floor of the Exchange to its client's accounts at the prevailing market price. The principle reason for conducting the Exchange offering following the effective date is that the underwriter must pay the listed company for the underwritten shares within five business days of the effective date of the SMF. The underwriter does not have the opportunity to terminate or market out of the underwriting agreement after the SMF is accepted by the regulatory authorities.

B. Underwriter's Options

The listed company is permitted to grant an underwriter an option to purchase additional shares of the company in consideration of underwriting the Exchange offering. There is no provision in Exchange Rule B.3.00 for transferring the underwriter's option to a sub-underwriter who is part of a selling group.

The number of shares which may be acquired pursuant to exercise of an underwriter's option must not be more than 50% of the number of shares underwritten. The maximum term for exercise of the option is two years. The exercise price per share in the first year of the option period must be at least equal to the underwriting price and, in the second year, must be increased by not less than 15% of the underwriting price.

AGENCY OFFERINGS

A. Best Efforts Offering

In a best efforts agency offering, the agent and the listed company agree on a minimum price per share below which the agent may not sell the shares being offered in an Exchange offering. The minimum price cannot be changed after the effective date of the SMF without filing an amendment to it with the Superintendent of Brokers and the Exchange. The Exchange may, however, require the agent and the company to renegotiate the minimum price prior to the effective date in the event that it is significantly higher or lower than the average market price of the company's shares during the five trading days preceding the effective date. The maximum permitted discount or premium of the minimum price per share in relation to the market price are as follows:

Market Price	Discount or Premium
up to $0.50	25%
$0.51 to $2.00	20%
over $2.00	15%

In any event, the minimum net price to the company must be $0.15 per share.

A best efforts offering involves an agent, using its best efforts, selling the shares of a listed company within a period of 180 calendar days from the effective date of the SMF. The Exchange offering is conducted by either crossing the shares on the Trading Floor of the Exchange to the agent's clients or selling the shares as the company's agent to clients of other Members in ordinary open market transactions which are referred to as open market distributions. The shares are sold at the prevailing market price for the company's shares at the time of sale. The net proceeds from the Exchange offering must be paid by the agent to the company within five business days of all of the shares being sold or the expiry of the 180 calendar day period, whichever occurs first. The agent generally has the opportunity to terminate the agency agreement at any time during the 180 calendar day offering period.

Where a listed company does not have sufficient working capital to carry out its intended exploration program or business plan as set out in the use of proceeds section of the SMF, the company and the agent may agree or the Exchange may require that a minimum number of shares be sold (known as the minimum subscription) as a pre-condition for the commencement of a best efforts agency offering. The portion of the offering relating to the minimum subscription must be conducted as a fixed price agency offering (described below).

B. Fixed Price Agency Offering

Unlike the best efforts offering or underwritten Exchange offering which may be conducted throughout the 180 calendar day period, an Exchange offering made by a fixed price agency offering must be made on a particular day within a period of 180 calendar days from the effective date of the SMF. The agent and the listed company will determine, with the consent of the Exchange, the day the Exchange offering is to be made, the offering day. The Exchange must be notified by the agent of the offering day no later than 11:00 a.m. on the trading day immediately preceding the offering day. A book is opened on the Trading Floor of the Exchange from the close of trading on the day preceding the offering day to 5:00 p.m. on the day preceding the offering day, and between 30 minutes and 5 minutes before the opening of trading on the offering day. The book is opened to receive subscription orders for the securities offered for sale under the SMF. On the offering day, the agent crosses the shares or units on the trading floor to its client's accounts at a fixed price. In other words, all shares or units must be sold at the same price in contrast to the best efforts offering or the underwritten Exchange offering where the company's shares are sold at the prevailing market prices at the time sales are made. The net proceeds from the fixed price agency offering must be paid by the agent to the listed company within five business days of the offering day. The agent cannot terminate its obligations under the agency agreement after the opening of trading on the offering day.

To determine the fixed price at which shares are sold in a fixed price agency offering, trading in the shares of the listed company is halted 30 minutes prior to the close of trading on the trading day immediately preceding the offering day. The Exchange determines, after 1:00 p.m. on the day preceding the offering day, the average market price of the company's shares by dividing the value of the shares traded by the volume of shares traded during the trading session on that day. The Exchange has sole discretion to determine the average market price in any other manner. The offering price of the shares must be agreed upon by the company and the agent but must not be at a discount of more than 10% below the average market price and, in any event, the minimum price net to the company must be $0.15 per share.

To determine the fixed price of units in a fixed price agency offering, the Exchange first determines the average market price of the listed company's shares in the same manner as discussed above. The unit price must be at a premium over the average market price. Where the number of share purchase warrants included in the unit is the same as the number of warrants required to acquire a further share, the minimum permitted premium in relation to the average market price is as follows:

Average Market Price	Premium
up to $1.50	10.0%
$1.51 to $2.50	7.5%
over $2.50	5.0%

Where the number of warrants included in the unit is not the same as the number of warrants required to acquire a further share, the premium of the unit price over the average market price must be calculated by multiplying the premium by the quotient of the number of warrants included in the unit divided by the number of warrants required to acquire a further share. For example, if a unit is comprised of one share and one share purchase warrant and two warrants are required to acquire a further share and the average market price of the company's shares is $1.00 per share, the unit price must be no less than $1.05, the average market price of $1.00 plus the product of the premium of $0.10 (10% of $1.00) multiplied by 1/2 (the number of warrants included in the unit divided by the number of warrants required to acquire a further share).

The minimum price net to the listed company from the sale of units in an Exchange offering must be $0.40 per unit unless a unit is comprised of more than one share in which case the minimum net price per unit must be the product of $0.40 multiplied by the number of shares comprising the unit. Where the offering price is less than $1.00 per unit, the Exchange offering must be for not less than 200,000 units. Where the offering price is equal to or greater than $1.00 per unit, the minimum number of units in the Exchange offering will be determined by the Exchange.

Where the units in a fixed price agency offering include transferable share purchase warrants, the minimum number of warrants offered must be 300,000, provided that the total number of shares which may be issued on exercise of the warrants must not exceed the total number of shares issued as part of the unit offering. As well, the maximum number of shares issued on exercise of non-transferable share purchase warrants must not exceed the total number of shares issued as part of the unit offering. While transferable share purchase warrants may be issued in bearer form, non-transferable share purchase warrants must be issued in the name of the holder with the words non-transferable printed on the warrant certificate.

The maximum term of share purchase warrants in a unit offering is two years which commences on the offering day. The Exchange will not permit an extension of the term of transferable warrants.

The Corporate and Financial Services Commission *In the Matter of Renata Mueller (a series A share purchase warrant holder of Kamad Silver Co. Ltd. (N.P.L.))* (January 13, 1981) did not overturn the decision of the Exchange to delist the shares of Kamad Silver Co. Ltd. (N.P.L.) (Kamad) as a result of Kamad extending the term of the transferable series A share purchase warrants issued under Kamad's SMF. The Commission found that the Exchange had provided Kamad with ample warning that it would oppose the extension of the warrants and had considered all material facts and the interests of all concerned in disapproving the warrant extension. The Exchange, in making the decision to delist the shares of Kamad, was concerned with those warrant holders who had sold their series A warrants prior to their expiry and the benefits they may have been denied by subsequently allowing an extension of the warrants. The Exchange currently includes a statement in its letter accepting an SMF that under no circumstances will the term of transferable share purchase warrants be extended.

The minimum exercise price per share of share purchase warrants included in the unit offering must be at least equal to the unit price. If the term of the warrant exceeds one year, the minimum exercise price per share must be increased in the second year by 15% of the average market price as determined by the Exchange. The warrant must not entitle the holder to acquire a further warrant upon its exercise.

Transferable share purchase warrants will be posted for trading on the Exchange unless the agent has advised the Exchange that less than 40 persons, including Members, hold such warrants. If the warrants are exercised to the point where the Exchange is of the opinion that there is insufficient distribution for an orderly market, the warrants may be traded on a cash basis only. Where the number of outstanding warrants is reduced to less than 75,000, the warrants will be delisted from the Exchange. In any event, during the last six trading days, the warrants will only trade for cash.

C. Guaranteed Agency Offering

An agent involved in a best efforts offering or a fixed price agency offering may undertake to purchase all of the shares or units, as the case may be, which are unsubscribed at the end of the Exchange offering. In consideration of the guarantee, the agent is entitled to a non-transferable share purchase warrant except in the case where the Exchange has ordered the company to conduct a best efforts offering. The agent may transfer an interest in the warrant to a sub-agent who is part of a selling group.

An agent's warrant must not be exercisable for more than 50% of the total number of shares or units in the share offering or unit offering, respectively. The maximum term of an agent's warrant must be limited to two years. In the case of a unit offering, the exercise term must not exceed the term of the public's share purchase warrants. Where a best efforts agency offering is guaranteed, the term of the agent's warrant commences on the earlier of the termination or completion of the Exchange offering and, in the case of a guaranteed fixed price agency offering, the term of the agent's warrant commences on the offering day.

In a fixed price share offering ,the exercise price per share of an agent's warrant in the first year of the warrant term must be at least equal to the average market price of the shares to be offered in the Exchange offering. In the second year of the warrant term, the exercise price must be increased by not less than 15% of the average market price. In the case of a fixed price unit offering, the exercise price per share of an agent's warrant in the first year must be at least equal to the price of the unit offered in the Exchange offering. In the second year of the warrant term, the exercise price must be increased by not less than 15% of the average market price of the share included in the unit.

In the case of a best efforts offering, the exercise price per share of an agent's warrant is determined at the earlier of the termination or completion of the best efforts offering. The exercise price in the first year is based on a price calculated by the Exchange by dividing the gross value of the shares sold by the agent in the Exchange offering by the actual number of shares sold (including the gross value and number of shares acquired by the agent pursuant to its guarantee obligation). The exercise price must be at least equal to the price calculated in this manner and must be increased in the second year by not less than 15% of that price.

Where the best efforts offering is guaranteed by the agent, the agent and the listed company must determine, with the consent of the Exchange, the day on which the Exchange offering is to commence. The agent must notify the Exchange of the commencement of the Exchange offering by no later than 1:00 p.m. on the trading day immediately preceding the day on which the Exchange offering is to commence. The Exchange offering may continue until the expiry of 180 calendar days from the effective date of the SMF. The agent is not permitted to terminate its obligations under the agency agreement once the Exchange offering has commenced.

D. Agent's Compensation

Exchange Rule B.3.00 provides that commissions payable to agents involved in Exchange offerings may be negotiated between the listed company and the agent, without restriction. The regulation of maximum commissions was removed by the Exchange in November, 1988.

GREENSHOE OPTIONS

In all Exchange offerings other than best efforts agency offerings, a greenshoe option may be granted to an underwriter or an agent to purchase additional securities of the listed company. The greenshoe option allows an underwriter or an agent the option, which may be exercised at the conclusion of the offering, to provide shares or units to the market where the offering has been over-subscribed. Such over-subscription privilege facilitates stability in the secondary trading market of the company's securities by helping to meet investor demand for the securities.

The material terms of the greenshoe option are provided in Exchange Rule B.3.00. The maximum number of securities which may be acquired on exercise of the greenshoe option is the lesser of *(a)* 15% of the number of shares or units sold in the Exchange offering and *(b)* the actual number of shares or units sold by an underwriter or an agent by way of over-subscription. The date for determining the over-subscription, in the case of a fixed price agency Exchange offering, is the offering day. In the case of an underwritten Exchange offering, the number of shares over-subscribed must be determined at the close of trading on the second day following the effective date of the SMF.

The maximum term of the greenshoe option is 60 calendar days commencing the offering day in the case of a fixed price agency Exchange offering, and 60 calendar days commencing the effective date of the SMF in the case of an underwritten Exchange offering. The exercise price of the option to acquire each additional share or unit must be the same as the net price to the company for each share or unit sold in the Exchange offering.

CHAPTER SEVEN

Shareholder Rights Offerings

GENERAL

In addition to the Exchange offering described in Chapter 6, a listed company may raise capital under a rights offering. The listed company issues rights to its existing shareholders which entitle them to purchase additional securities of the company through the exercise of the rights. Although the rights are issued at no cost to the shareholders, they are posted for trading on the Exchange and the shareholders may sell them through the facilities of the Exchange. If the shareholders choose to exercise the rights, the purchase price for the additional securities is paid to the company.

The offering of rights to shareholders as well as the issuance of securities upon exercise of the rights are exempted from Part 7 of the *Securities Act*, the prospectus qualification provisions, by virtue of paragraph 55(2)(7) in the *Act*. However, the Securities Commission and the Canadian Securities Administrators have formulated Local Policy Statement No. 3-05 (February 1, 1987) and Uniform Act Policy Statement No. 2-05, respectively, under which rights offerings must be conducted in British Columbia. If a listed company wishes all of its shareholders to participate in the trading and exercise of the rights, it must comply with the applicable securities regulations of each jurisdiction in which its shareholders reside. Furthermore, if the rights are purchased through the facilities of the Exchange by residents outside British Columbia, the rights offering must comply with the applicable securities laws of the residents' jurisdiction in order for them to exercise the rights.

The following discussion focuses on the applicable rules and policies of the Exchange and the Securities Commission respecting rights offerings conducted through the facilities of the Exchange to British Columbia residents only. It does not deal with circumstances where a listed company has a principal trading area outside British Columbia or where British Columbia residents hold less than 5% of the outstanding shares of the company; these circumstances are specifically dealt with in Local Policy Statement No. 3-05.

EXCHANGE RULES

Part F of Exchange Rule B.3.00 sets out the Exchange's requirements for conducting a rights offering where the offering is made to holders of the class of shares of a listed company which is posted for trading on the Exchange. Unless otherwise indicated, the following discussion is derived from Part F of Rule B.3.00.

A minimum of one right must be issued for each outstanding share of the listed company. The rights may entitle the holder to purchase shares or units of the company.

The subscription price to acquire a share upon the exercise of rights must be less than the market price of the listed company's shares on the day the rights offering documentation is accepted for filing by the Exchange. The price, however, must not be significantly less than the following maximum discounts from the market price:

Market Price	Maximum Discount
up to $0.50	50%
$0.51 to $2.00	40%
over $2.00	30%

Where units of the listed company may be acquired upon the exercise of rights, the minimum subscription price per unit must be the greater of $0.40 or a price which is determined by discounting the market price as set out above and adding a premium to the discounted price. The Special Policy Committee has recommended that the minimum subscription price per unit be reduced to $0.25 to encourage more use of this financing mechanism by inactive companies. Where the number of share purchase warrants included in the unit is equal to the number of warrants required to acquire one additional share, the following minimum premiums must be added to the discounted price:

Discounted Price	Premium
up to $1.50	10.0%
$1.51 to $2.50	7.5%
over $2.50	5.0%

Where the number of share purchase warrants included in the unit is not equal to the number of warrants required to acquire one additional share, the minimum premium to be added to the discounted price must be calculated by multiplying the premium set out above by the quotient of the number of warrants included in the unit divided by the number of warrants required to acquire one additional share.

The minimum exercise price of the share purchase warrants must not be less than the discounted price as described above. If the exercise period of the warrants is for a term of two years, the minimum exercise price must be increased in the second year by a premium of 15% of the discounted price.

As an example, assume that the listed company wishes to conduct a rights offering of 500,000 units, each unit consisting of one share and one share purchase warrant which entitles the holder to purchase one additional share for every two such warrants at any time within a two year period. Assume further that the market price of the company's shares on the date the rights offering material is accepted for filing by the Exchange is $1.00 per share and that the company wishes to price the unit at the maximum discounted price. To the discounted price of $0.60 (the market price of $1.00 less the maximum discount of 40%) would be added $0.03, the amount obtained by multiplying the premium of $0.06 (10% of the discounted price) by 1/2 (the number of warrants included in the unit divided by the number of warrants required to acquire an additional share). Every two warrants would entitle the holder to acquire one additional share at exercise prices of $0.60 in the first year (the discounted price) and $0.69 in the second year (the discounted price plus a 15% premium).

The term of the rights offering must not exceed 30 days from the record date (described below), where the listed company has specified that a minimum amount must be raised pursuant to the offering, or 90 days from the record date, where no minimum amount has been specified. The expiry date of the rights may only be extended where, due to circumstances beyond the control of the company, delivery of the rights to the shareholders has been prevented. Such an extension is only available where the rights have not yet been traded on the Exchange and the Superintendent of Brokers consents to the extension.

Where the listed company requires a certain amount of funds for a specific use (for example, to conduct a recommended phase of exploration work), a minimum subscription must be determined by the company and this subscription must be guaranteed by a person or company having, in the opinion of the Exchange, the financial ability to satisfy the standby guarantee. The Exchange will generally require some written confirmation that the guarantor has funds available to it to satisfy the guarantee, such as a statement of net worth attested to by the guarantor or a bank letter of credit. The Special Policy Committee has recommended that the need for a guaranteed minimum subscription be waived where the rights offering is being conducted as part of a reactivation by an inactive company.

In consideration of the standby guarantee, the listed company may give a bonus to the guarantor in the form of a non-transferable share purchase warrant entitling the guarantor to acquire shares of the company equal in number to not more than 40% of the total number of shares which may have to be acquired pursuant to the guarantee. The warrant must not exceed a six month period from the date on which the guarantee may be required. The subscription proceeds in satisfaction of the guarantee must be paid to the company within seven days of the expiry date of the rights. The exercise price of the warrant must not be less than the subscription price to exercise the rights.

Assume, for example, that the listed company proposing the rights offering of 500,000 units at $0.63 per unit requires minimum proceeds of $126,000.00. The guarantor must guarantee the subscription of 200,000 units to provide proceeds of $126,000.00. The guarantor would be entitled to a non-transferable share purchase warrant to acquire 80,000 shares (40% of the 200,000 shares included in the 200,000 units) exercisable for a six month period at a price of not less than $0.63 per share.

The subscribers to a rights offering may subscribe to more than the number of rights they are entitled to where the listed company so provides. The over-subscription privilege must be based on a pro rating formula acceptable to both the Exchange and the Superintendent of Brokers. An acceptable pro rata formula (set out in Local Policy Statement No. 3-05) allows each shareholder to acquire the number of securities available through unexercised rights that is obtained by multiplying the total number of securities available through all unexercised rights by the quotient of the number of rights exercised by the shareholder divided by the aggregate number of rights exercised by all shareholders. The standby guarantor may acquire all securities not subscribed, under the over-subscription privilege.

The Superintendent of Brokers will generally object to an insider of the listed company providing a standby guarantee if the shareholders are not given the privilege to over-subscribe. Local Policy Statement No. 3-05 discusses the view of the Superintendent that insiders may have access to information not available to others which may provide insights into the company's affairs. Accordingly, the Superintendent is concerned with any provision in the rights offering which may provide an insider with an advantage over other shareholders in increasing the insider's shareholdings.

As discussed above, the term of the rights offering commences from the record date. Those shareholders whose names appear on the listed company's register of shareholders on the record date will be entitled to receive the rights. Any person who acquires the company's shares at any time within four business days prior to the record date will not be entitled to receive the rights. The fourth business day prior to the record date is referred to as the ex-rights date and notice of the ex-rights date must be given for at least two clear trading days prior to the ex-rights date.

The rights issued under the rights offering must be transferable and will be called for trading on the Exchange on the ex-rights date. The rights will trade under normal settlement rules of five business days until the last six trading days, and during this period the rights may only trade on a cash basis. In other words, payment for the rights must be made immediately rather than within five business days after the purchase.

Where the rights offering is of units, the term of the share purchase warrants included in the unit will commence from the expiry date of the rights and must not exceed six months for a Venture Company and two years for all other listed companies. The warrant cannot be a piggy-back warrant, that is, it must not entitle the holder to acquire a further warrant upon its exercise.

The rights offering of units must consist of not less than 300,000 transferable share purchase warrants and the number of shares acquired on exercise of such warrants must not exceed the number of shares issued as part of the unit offering. The warrants will be posted and called for trading upon completion of the rights offering provided not less than 40 persons, including Members, hold warrants. The listed company must submit shareholder distribution lists to the Exchange disclosing the number of persons who have exercised their rights.

If, in the Exchange's opinion, there is insufficient distribution of the outstanding transferable share purchase warrants for an orderly market, the Exchange may declare that the warrants must be traded on a cash basis only. In any event, during the last six trading days the warrants will only trade for cash. In the event the number of outstanding transferable warrants is reduced to less than 75,000 due to exercise of the warrants, the outstanding warrants will be delisted from trading on the Exchange.

Where the share purchase warrants included in the rights offering of units are not transferable, the number of shares which may be issued by their exercise must not exceed the number of shares issued as part of the unit rights offering and the certificates representing the non-transferable share purchase warrants must be issued in the name of the holder with the words non-transferable printed on them.

Local Policy Statement No. 3-05 provides that, following acceptance of the rights offering material by the Superintendent of Brokers, the listed company must notify unregistered shareholders not later than three business days after such acceptance by publishing a notice in at least one issue of a daily newspaper published and circulating in the City of Vancouver. The notice must be addressed to the shareholders and contain the dates of commencement and termination of the offering and the material particulars of the offering. In addition, the offering must not commence until the expiration of seven business days after the

Superintendent has accepted the rights offering material and, as discussed above, the shares of the listed company must trade ex-rights commencing four business days prior to the record date, provided two clear trading days notice of the ex-rights date has been given. The earliest at which these events may occur may be summarized as follows:

Business Day 1 -   acceptance of rights offering by the Exchange and the Superintendent of Brokers;

Business Day 2 -   notice of rights offering in daily newspaper;

Business Day 5 -   ex-rights date (so long as business days 3 and 4 are trading days) and the date for listing the rights on the Exchange;

Business Day 9 -   record date;

Calendar Day 40 -   maximum expiry date if rights offering has a minimum subscription;

Calendar Day 100 - maximum expiry date if rights offering has no minimum subscription.

THE APPROVAL PROCESS

The listed company's rights offering documentation must be reviewed by the Exchange and the Superintendent of Brokers and those other jurisdictions whose rights offering regulations are being complied with. The Exchange is not bound by any time period within which to provide comments to the company on the rights offering material. In the case of the Superintendent, paragraph 55(2)(7) of the *Act* provides that, if the Superintendent objects to the rights offering, the Superintendent should inform the company within ten days of the company giving written notice of the rights offering. Notice of the rights offering may be provided to the Superintendent in a covering letter which refers to the accompanying rights offering material. In practice, the Superintendent will provide some response to the listed company on the rights offering documentation and, in any event, the company may not proceed with the offering until the Exchange has been provided with the consent of the Superintendent to the rights offering.

In practice, the rights offering material is filed contemporaneously with all regulatory authorities. Comments on the material are generally communicated in writing to the filing solicitor. When all comments have been dealt with to the satisfaction of the authorities, the Exchange will accept the rights offering documentation for filing.

DOCUMENTATION REQUIREMENTS

Exchange Rule B.3.45, Securities Commission Local Policy Statement No. 3-05 and Uniform Act Policy Statement No. 2-05 set out the information and documentation to be provided to the Exchange and the Superintendent of Brokers for a proposed rights offering. The main document, to be filed with the Exchange and the Superintendent and to be provided to all registered shareholders, is the rights offering circular, which must disclose the following information:

- the material facts of the offering, including:
  - the number of rights to be issued for each outstanding share;
  - the total number of shares or units to be offered in relation to the total number of outstanding shares;
  - the number of rights required to subscribe for each share or unit;
  - the subscription price to exercise the rights;
  - the record date;
  - the expiry date;
  - the procedure for subscribing to exercise the rights;
  - the procedure for selling or transferring the rights;
  - the dollar amount of the minimum subscription, if any;
  - the guarantor, if any, and the terms and amount of the guarantee;
  - the terms of the pro rata over-subscription, if any;
  - the use of proceeds from the offering;
  - the name of the company's registrar and transfer agent administering the offering;
  - the jurisdictions in which the offering is to be made and any material procedures required to be followed by those jurisdictions if they differ from the procedures applicable in British Columbia;
  - payments to be made to any person or company in connection with the offering;
  - the terms of the warrants to be issued, if any, on exercise of the rights;
- a brief description of the listed company's business activities, material asset acquisitions and dispositions and other material facts;
- disclosure concerning the company's ongoing programs and summaries of technical reports filed with the Superintendent of Brokers in accordance with Local Policy Statement No. 3-05 if the reports have not been distributed to the shareholders;
- the date of the last annual general meeting and particulars of any extraordinary general meeting held since the last annual general meeting;
- any change in the directors and senior officers since the last annual general meeting;

- particulars known to the directors of any transfer of shares which has materially affected the control of the company since the last meeting of shareholders or a statement that no such particulars are known;
- disclosure of all material transactions likely to be consummated by the conclusion of the offering;
- where no minimum subscription has been provided for, disclosure of the risk that insufficient proceeds may be available from subscription to enable the aims and objectives of the offering to be carried out; and
- where a minimum subscription has been provided by a standby underwriting which contains a market out clause, disclosure of the market out provision and of the arrangement made to ensure that the subscriptions are returned to the subscribers in full in the event that the minimum amount is not obtained.

The Exchange will require the listed company to file a Filing Statement unless it is satisfied that all information which would otherwise be disclosed in the Filing Statement is included in the rights offering circular. In addition, Securities Commission Local Policy Statement No. 3-05 provides that the Superintendent of Brokers may require the rights offering to be conducted by a prospectus or SMF where: *(a)* the offering, if completely subscribed, would result in an increase of more than 50% in the number of shares outstanding, *(b)* the offering is for the purpose of financing a major new undertaking or involves a change of control within twelve months of the listed company completing its first distribution of shares to the public, or *(c)* the listed company has not yet completed the programs disclosed in the use of proceeds section of the prospectus under which the company became a reporting company or has not yet reported on the results of the program. It is not clear, in these circumstances, to whom the prospectus or SMF must be given, nor is it clear if anyone obtains the special rescission rights made available by s.114 of the *Securities Act*.

In summary, the following documents must be filed with the Exchange along with the appropriate filing fee:

- a Filing Statement, if required, and the rights offering circular;
- a specimen rights subscription certificate and warrant certificate, if any;
- a copy of the company's most recent financial statements, if they are not already filed;
- where a standby guarantee is required, a written commitment from the guarantor to exercise the guaranteed portion within seven days of expiration of the offer, together with satisfactory evidence of the guarantor's ability to carry out the provisions of the guarantee; and
- the Superintendent's consent to the offering being made.

The documents to be filed with the Superintendent of Brokers together with the prescribed filing fee are as follows:

- a covering letter which includes formal notice to the Superintendent of Brokers of the offering and a list of the other jurisdictions in Canada in which the offering is being made;
- the rights offering circular;
- a specimen rights subscription certificate;
- where a standby guarantee is required, the plans for subsequent distribution of the securities so acquired together with evidence of the guarantor's ability to carry out the provisions of the guarantee;
- a copy of the company's most recent financial statements, if they are not already filed;
- a copy of the company's latest annual report and annual general meeting information circular, if they are not already filed;
- the minutes of the most recent annual general meeting and any extraordinary general meeting held subsequent to the annual general meeting;
- where proceeds from the offering are to be used to fund specific programs, appropriate technical reports conforming to the specifications under the *Securities Act* (for example, Securities Commission Local Policy Statements Nos. 3-01 and 3-04 (February 1, 1987)); and
- a statement signed by a senior officer of the company to the effect that there have been no material changes in the affairs of the company since the date of the last audited financial statements delivered to shareholders or that all such changes have been disclosed in the rights offering circular and that there are no undisclosed material transactions currently under negotiation which are likely to require a news release prior to expiry of the rights offering.

In general, listed companies file the same documentation with the Exchange and the Superintendent of Brokers.

Following the record date, the listed company must mail each registered shareholder the rights offering circular, the rights subscription certificate and copies of the company's last annual report, audited financial statements and notice of the last annual meeting, if they have not already been provided to the shareholders.

CHAPTER EIGHT

Private Placements

GENERAL

A listed company, by virtue of the provisions of its listing agreement with the Exchange, must give the Exchange prompt notice of any proposed material change and obtain the Exchange's prior approval for that change. The listing agreement defines a material change to include any proposed share issuance and therefore any private placement. In this connection, it should be observed that the provisions of Listings Policy Statement No. 9 do not create exemptions for smaller private placements. The share issuance exemption in that Policy Statement only exempts certain share issuances involving an acquisition or disposition of assets at arm's length to listed companies.

The Exchange has two, quite separate Listings Policy Statements which deal with private placements. The first, Listings Policy Statement No. 11, deals with the private placement of equity shares, that is, a voting share of a listed company. The second Policy Statement is Listings Policy Statement No. 21 which deals with the private placement of convertible securities, defined as securities which are convertible into equity shares.

A third area entailed in both of these categories is the regulation of both types of private placements, where they are undertaken by an agent or broker. The latter placements are called brokered private placements. The requirements associated with these types of placements are contained in the last part of Listings Policy Statement No. 11.

Essentially, a private placement is defined as a private underwriting of a listed company's securities where the private underwriting is exempted from Part 7 of the *Securities Act*, the prospectus qualification provisions, by virtue of: any of the exemptions found in the *Securities Act*; the Regulation to the *Securities Act*; or by a favourable order made pursuant to the provisions of s.59 of the *Securities Act*. The applicable exemptions in the first and second categories listed above are the exempt institution exemption, the exempt purchaser exemption, the $97,000.00 exemption, the $25,000.00 purchaser exemption, the 50 purchaser exemption and the friends and relatives exemption.

EQUITY SHARE PRIVATE PLACEMENTS

A. Public Disclosure

Any private placement of equity shares is deemed by the Exchange to constitute a material change in the affairs of a listed company and therefore the Exchange requires a listed company to issue a news release announcing the placement on the day that the parties agree to the terms of the placement. This day, a particularly important day in terms of the subject Listings Policy Statement, is called the agreement day. The news release, it should be noted, may not be issued for the purpose of locking in the placement price before all parties have agreed to the placement. If the listed company does not issue this required news release, the Exchange will refuse to approve the placement although it should not, from a common sense point of view, have any reason to disapprove a placement where the market price of the underwritten shares has remained the same or depreciated in the intervening period.

The news release must contain all the material particulars of the placement. Typically this would indicate the type and number of securities underwritten, the underwriting price together with a brief description of the proposed use of the placement proceeds. If options or warrants are included in the placement, then the number of these should be specified, as well as the number of equity shares which are callable, and the exercise term and exercise price. If a finders fee or commission is involved, then full particulars of these should also be disclosed in the same release. The fact that the private placement is subject to Exchange, and if required, shareholder approval should also be disclosed.

In addition to the news release described above, the listed company may be required to file a *Securities Act* Form 27, a material change report, with the Securities Commission if the private placement, under the provisions of s.67 of the *Act*, constitutes a material change in the affairs of the listed company. The news release issuance requirement associated with the material change under the *Act* should be satisfied by the listed company's compliance with the Exchange's news release requirements so long as the nature and substance of the material change is disclosed. A Form 27 must be filed within 10 days of the occurrence of the material change. A copy of the Form 27 must also be filed with the Exchange.

The listed company is required to issue a news release upon the completion of the private placement, although, in actual practice, most listed companies rely on the Exchange Notice which is issued by the Exchange after its final approval has been given. Alternatively, if the placement has not been approved by the Exchange, or otherwise has been terminated, a news release must be issued immediately. The comments noted above with respect to the filing with the Securities Commission of a Form 27 should also be borne in mind in these latter cases.

B. Pricing

The minimum net price to the treasury of a listed company is $0.15 unless the company's shares have been consolidated within the three months prior to the private placement, in which case the minimum net price per share is the greater of $0.15 and $0.07 multiplied by the share consolidation ratio. For example, if the share consolidation was effected on a 1:4 basis, then the minimum price per share restriction would be $0.28 in the three months following the share consolidation. The minimum underwriting price, that is the per share price paid by the investors, is calculated by taking the closing price of the listed company's shares on the agreement day (if this day falls on an Exchange trading day) or the last trading day preceding the agreement day (if the agreement day does not take place on an Exchange trading day) and subtracting the following discounts.

Closing Price	Maximum Discount
up to $0.50	25%
$0.51 to $2.00	20%
over $2.00	15%

If the average closing price of the listed company's shares during the 2 week period preceding the agreement day exceeds the actual closing price on the agreement day, or the last trading day prior to the agreement day, by a percentage greater than the appropriate discount percentage noted above, then that average trading price must be used for calculating the underwriting price instead of the actual closing price. This particular provision is designated to prevent artificially low prices to be paid for private placement shares.

One unwritten policy of the Exchange regarding the pricing of private placements was discussed by the Securities Commission in *In the Matter of Argonaut Resources Ltd.*, (November 5, 1987). In that case, the listed company, Argonaut Resources Ltd., agreed to issue certain shares by private placement essentially at the same time as a major asset acquisition was announced. The private placees had no connection, according to the facts recited in the decision, to the vendors of the major asset. Argonaut Resources Ltd. argued that the Exchange's unwritten one transaction rule should be applied to enable the Exchange to grant its acceptance of the private placement. The Exchange declined to do so, positing that the one transaction rule did not apply. The rule permits an exception to the general rule requiring private placement shares to be issued at a price which reflects all material information about the affairs of the listed company in the case where a major acquisition and a private placement represent, in substance, one transaction. The Exchange based its decision on the fact that the acquisition and the placement did not go hand in hand in the sense that the placees in question were not part of the vending group. The Securities Commission, while not ruling on the question of whether the facts evidenced a breach of the insider trading provisions of the *Act*, requested the Exchange to re-examine the one transaction rule, a re-examination which, at the time of writing this book, had not been completed. On December 4, 1987 however, the Exchange publicly announced its interim guidelines which would be in effect pending the re-examination. These guidelines were expressed as follows:

- incentive stock options granted to directors or employees of the listed company based on the pre-announcement price will not be permitted prior to public disclosure of the material transaction; and
- private placements will be accepted if, and only if, the purchasers are the vendors (excluding insiders of the listed company) or their associates; the private placement funds have been committed subject only to regulatory approval; the acquisition was only available to the listed company if the specific funding was itself immediately available; and the private placement funding was specifically allocated and necessary for the purpose of closing the transaction.

The Exchange will not be favourably disposed to approving such a private placement if warrants having an exercise price based on the pre-announcement price are granted as part of the placement. It should be noted that the Exchange will find incentive stock options and warrants acceptable if a post-announcement exercise price is used. In these cases, the average post-announcement closing price over a certain trading day period will have to be used.

Listings Policy Statement No. 22, which deals with reverse take-overs (discussed in Chapter 4), does provide that the Exchange may accept a private placement which is priced prior to public disclosure of the reverse take-over where the placement is integral to the transaction. There is no suggestion that the placement must be made to persons involved in the reverse take-over and not to insiders of the listed company. Additionally, Listings Policy Statement No. 22 provides that no stock options may be granted by a listed company involved in a reverse take-over until at least thirty days have transpired from closing of the reverse take-over and resumption of trading of the listed company's shares. At the time of writing this book, it appears that the Exchange is applying these provisions of Listings Policy Statement No. 22 to all transactions (not just reverse take-overs) involving the pricing of private placements and stock options prior to the public announcement of a material transaction and that the guidelines announced by the Exchange on December 4, 1987, as discussed above, have been superceded.

C. Shareholder Approval

The shareholders of a listed company are required to approve any private placement of equity shares, as well as the granting of any options or warrants in connection with such a placement, if the number of underwritten shares to be issued to one investor, or group of investors who intend to vote their shares as a group, is equal to or greater than 20% of the number of the company's shares outstanding after giving effect to the issuance of the underwritten shares. Shareholder approval is also required where the issuance of the underwritten shares may result in a change in the effective control of the listed company, create a control block or otherwise is part of a transaction having either of these two results. Note that shareholder approval is not required when the private placement is made on a non-arm's length basis, unless it involves a change of control of the listed company.

D. Options and Warrants

Non-transferable share purchase warrants or options representing a call on a certain amount of the listed company's treasury stock may be granted if it is essential to the making of the private placement. The total number of treasury shares which may be made subject to option cannot exceed the number of underwritten shares. Options must not exceed a term of two years from the day on which the investor and the company execute a binding agreement pursuant to which the investor becomes irrevocably bound, which agreement is made subject only to regulatory approval. The exercise price of the option in the first year must be at least equal to the underwriting price. In the second year of the option, the exercise price must be increased by a minimum of 15% over the underwriting price.

E. Hold Period

Listings Policy Statements Nos. 11 and 21 provide that in the absence of a specific hold period imposed under the provisions of the *Securities Act*, or by an order made by the Superintendent of Brokers, the underwritten shares must not be sold or otherwise disposed of for a period of one year from the day on which the company and the investor become irrevocably committed to the placement, subject only to regulatory approval. All shares issued in such circumstances must bear a legend setting forth the applicable hold period. Any shares issued on exercise of options or warrants are also subject to these requirements; the hold period is identical to the hold period associated with the underwritten shares. It should be noted that the Exchange hold period policy is not applied in the case of placements involving exempt institutions or exempt purchasers. With the coming into force, on February 1, 1987, of the new *Act* and its creation of the so-called closed system, the Exchange has provided in Listings Policy Statement No. 11 that it will not object to trades made in lettered stock so long as the trades are made within the closed system. The Exchange also permits the resale to the public of private placement shares if they are offered pursuant to an SMF or prospectus with a Member acting as agent.

F. Exchange Approval Process

The approval process for the private placement of equity shares involves two stages. First, on or promptly after the agreement day, the listed company must file a special notice with the Exchange. This notice will be reviewed by the staff of the Listings Department and must include in the following order:

- the name of the listed company,
- the statutory exemption from prospectus qualification provisions being relied upon,
- the number of underwritten shares,
- the proposed underwriting price per share,
- the names and addresses of the investors,
- the proposed use of proceeds,
- particulars of any finder's fee,
- particulars of any options or warrants granted,
- particulars of any other proposed material changes in the affairs of the company, and
- particulars of any unusual features of the transaction (i.e. flow-through shares).

This notice, it should be observed, may not be filed to freeze the price of a private placement before the actual agreement day. The Exchange, under the Policy Statement, is obliged to accept or reject the company's notice within five business days of receiving it.

Providing the Exchange has accepted this notice for filing, the second stage to the approval process involves the listed company making a second filing within thirty days of the acceptance by the Exchange of the company's first notice. There are two filing procedures which may be used by the listed company. The first procedure is the regular filing procedure and if this particular method is chosen, these documents must be filed, together with the applicable filing fee, as part of the second filing:

- a true copy of the private placement agreement or subscription agreement;
- a Filing Statement disclosing the material terms of the private placement unless this requirement has been waived by the Exchange;
- a legal opinion, if requested by the Exchange, that the distribution is exempt from the prospectus qualifications provisions of the *Act;*
- a signed statement by each investor stating that the securities are not being acquired as a result of any material information about the affairs of the listed company not publicly disclosed unless such statement is required to be, and has been, filed with the Superintendent of Brokers;
- an undertaking by each investor to the Exchange agreeing to hold the shares for one year from the payment day, which is defined as the date upon which the company and the investor become irrevocably committed to the placement, subject only to regulatory approval, unless this undertaking is required to be, and has been, filed with the Superintendent of Brokers;
- confirmation that the funds have been advanced to the listed company or in trust for the company's benefit pending regulatory approval; and
- any other information which may be required by the Exchange.

If the certified filing procedure is used, then, in addition to the appropriate fee, the listed company must submit a private placement questionnaire and undertaking (this document comprises Appendix 1 to the Listings Policy Statement) together with the declaration of certified filing and summary form (Appendix 2 to the Listings Policy Statement), duly completed by a director or officer of the listed company. When this procedure is used, the Exchange will automatically accept the filing. This is not the case if the regular filing procedure is used as the Exchange makes a complete review of the documents filed prior to acceptance, making a selective review of certified filings on an after-the-fact basis. If it determines that a particular filing is not acceptable, the Exchange may declare that this results in a breach of the company's listing agreement, probably ruling that the company cannot use the certified filing procedure in the future.

If the listed company does not file this information within the required period of time, then the Exchange will deem the placement to be abandoned. From a practice point of view, if the circumstances are such that a complete filing cannot be made for good reason, then the Exchange should be notified of this prior to the expiry of the 30 day period as in most cases it will grant an extension to the period of time for the filing, so long as all of the private placement funds have been provided to the listed company and substantially all of the required documents are filed. If the placement is abandoned, then a subsequent private placement with any of the original investors at a lower price per share will be refused by the Exchange for a ninety day period commencing from the date of the first notice filed by the listed company with the Exchange.

CONVERTIBLE SECURITY PRIVATE PLACEMENTS

A. General Requirements

The Exchange's regulatory rules and procedural structure associated with the private placement of equity shares have been adapted to the private placement of convertible securities. Thus the disclosure rules are similar and the minimum conversion price is tied to the market price of the listed company's shares. There are, however, some merit review standards incorporated into Listings Policy Statement No. 21. These standards (the jurisdiction for which were approved by the Corporate and Financial Services Commission *In the Matter of Bali Exploration Ltd.*, (July 27, 1976)), set out a framework indicating when the Exchange will accept or prohibit the issuance of debt securities by a particular listed company. The Policy Statement indicates that the Exchange will not permit a debt security issuance where, in substance, the listed company cannot afford it, even where an investor may have otherwise agreed to take down the issuance and has accepted the risk that the debt and interest may not be repaid. The Policy Statement requires the listed company to satisfy the Exchange, before it will accept the placement, that it has reasonable prospects of being in a financial position to satisfy all recurring payment obligations such as periodic interest, principal or dividend payments and, as well, that it is able to pay or refinance any redemption or principal repayment obligations. Moreover, the Exchange will not approve the issuance of a convertible security, even if both of these tests are met to the satisfaction of the Exchange, where interest payments are made convertible into the company's equity shares or where the ability to service and repay a debt obligation is dependent upon the exercise of options or warrants granted as part of the placement. In addition, where the redemption or principal payment obligation is dependent upon the conversion of the security into equity shares, the Exchange will refuse to accept the filing.

B. Public Disclosure

As in the case of equity private placements, the issuance of convertible securities by a listed company is deemed by the terms of Listings Policy Statement No. 21 to constitute a material change in the affairs of that listed company. Accordingly, the company must issue and disseminate a news release detailing the nature and substance of the placement. Matters such as the dollar amount and number of securities, the obligations proposed to be entered, together with the material particulars of conversion terms, options, warrants and finder's fees should be disclosed.

The same rules pertaining to abandonment, Exchange rejection and other terminations associated with equity share private placements, and *Securities Act* Form 27 requirements, apply to placements of convertible securities.

C. Pricing

Convertible preferred shares, convertible debentures or other convertible securities (which include convertible loans) are customarily issued at a face amount and accordingly there are no special Exchange rules relating to issuance prices contained in Listings Policy Statement No. 21. One could argue that these types of securities may be issued at a discount, as is the case with equity shares, where such a discount is otherwise permitted by law, as the specifically regulated prices in the Policy Statement only relate to the conversion terms of the securities involved as well as the maximum number and exercise prices associated with options and warrants.

The conversion price per share in any twelve month period subsequent to the payment day, which again is defined as the day on which the company and the investor become irrevocably committed to the placement, subject only to regulatory approval, must not be less than the average closing price of the listed company's equity shares over the two week period preceding the agreement day. The conversion price per share in each subsequent year must be escalated by not less than $0.05 per share in the conversion price range up to and including $0.50 per share, not less than $0.10 per share in the conversion price range above $0.50 and up to and including $1.00 per share and not less than $0.25 per share in the conversion price range above $1.00 per share. The minimum conversion price in the first year must not be less than $0.15 per share except in the case of the listed company's first placement of convertible securities following a share consolidation of the company's shares within three months prior to the date of the listed company giving its first notice of the private placement to the Exchange, in which case the minimum conversion price must be the greater of $0.15 or $0.07 multiplied by the consolidation ratio.

The Exchange generally will not approve the private placement of convertible securities where the conversion terms permit conversion into the listed company's equity shares for a period exceeding five years. The exception is exempt companies. The Exchange may, however, allow modifications to these terms, depending on the company's stage of development.

D. Shareholder Approval

The shareholder approval requirement associated with the private placement of equity shares applies to private placements of convertible securities. That is, if the number of shares issuable on the conversion of the securities to one investor or group of investors who intend to vote their shares as a group is equal to or exceeds 20% of the number of the listed company's shares outstanding (after including the shares which would be issued on conversion and on the exercise of any options or warrants), then shareholder approval is required, including approval for any of the options or warrants. Shareholder approval is also required if the issuance of shares on conversion or exercise of options or warrants may otherwise result in a change of effective control or the creation of a control block.

E. Options and Warrants

Options, or share purchase warrants, may be issued to the investor if they are essential for the private placement. The provisions of Listings Policy Statement No. 21 permit both the issuance of securities convertible into units comprised of a share and a share purchase warrant and the issuance of a convertible security together with a detachable warrant. The total number of shares which may be issued on the exercise of the warrants, all of which must be non-transferable, is not permitted to exceed the number of shares which may be issued on the conversion of the security. Where the security is convertible into units, then the exercise term of the warrant may not exceed the earlier of the term of the convertible security for conversion into equity shares or two years from the date of conversion of the convertible security. Where warrants are issued along with the convertible security itself, then the term of that warrant must not exceed the earlier of the term of conversion of the convertible security or two years from the payment day. The restrictions dealing with the minimum exercise price of warrants issued in connection with the private placement of convertible securities are identical to those which apply in the case of equity share private placements.

F. Hold Period

The hold period restrictions which apply to the convertible securities or any shares issued either on the exercise of a conversion term or pursuant to a warrant or option are identical to those which apply in the case of equity share private placements.

G. Exchange Approval Process

The two-stage approval process utilized by the Exchange in the case of the private placement of equity shares applies, in an almost identical way, to the private placement of convertible securities. Thus both the regular filing procedure or the special certified filing procedure could be used. The main difference is that, as part of its first filing with the Exchange, a listed company must describe how it is going to be able to make any required periodic payments and how it is to be capable of redeeming or paying out the principal debt obligation. Similarly, the provisions of the Exchange's equity share private placement policy, dealing with failing to make the second filing with the Exchange, apply in cases where the security being privately placed is a convertible one.

BROKERED PRIVATE PLACEMENTS

The final sections of Listings Policy Statement No. 11 set out the Exchange's requirements where the private placement, whether of equity shares or convertible securities, is undertaken by an agent or a broker on behalf of the listed company. It is important to recognize that the Superintendent of Brokers' Notice (January 30, 1986) indicated that non-registered agents who reside in British Columbia are not entitled to receive a commission for acting as an agent or broker on a placement since this would, in his view, involve a breach of the registration provisions contained in s.20 of the *Securities Act*. This same caveat should be borne in mind in situations where the agent or broker is resident in another province or state in the United States of America since most of those jurisdictions have registration provisions similar to those found in the *Act*. It should be noted that with respect to the *Act*, and notwithstanding the Superintendent's warning, paragraph 31(2)(3) of the *Act* does create a registration exemption where the trade is isolated and not made in the course of successive transactions.

At the time of writing this book, the Exchange is proposing to amend Exchange Rule F.2.25.2 to include reference to Rule F.2.30, thereby providing that no commissions or fees in connection with the sale or placement of securities of a listed company may be paid to an employee, officer, director or partner of a corporation or partnership which is not a Member but performs the same functions as a Member. In other words, commissions and fees for arranging a private placement may be paid only to a Member or entity performing the same functions as a Member, no matter where it is resident, and not to an individual salesman, employee, director or officer.

The three areas of the non-brokered private placement policy requirements which have been revised by the Exchange to meet the needs of the brokered private placement are the Exchange approval procedure, the news release requirements and the pricing provision.

With respect to the approval procedure, the listed company must make the standard first filing except that the name and address of the agent must be provided instead of the names and addresses of the investors. Within thirty days of the Exchange accepting the listed company's notice, it must file the same documentation as is required for a non-brokered placement together with a copy of the agency agreement. Failure to do so will mean that the Exchange will not accept a subsequent notice from the company disclosing an agency agreement between the listed company and the same agent at a price per share less than that specified in the first notice, unless ninety days have elapsed from the date of the first notice.

With respect to the news release requirements, the same type of news release requirements apply to brokered placements as do those which apply to non-brokered placements. Similarly the same comments with respect to the *Act* Form 27 apply.

Turning to the pricing of a brokered private placement, there is a substantial difference between the two sets of rules. In the case of the non-brokered private placement, a purchase price cannot be finalized until all parties to the placement have agreed to proceed. In the case of a brokered placement, the price must be negotiated between the listed company and the agent beforehand, taking into account the closing price and maximum discount rules. Upon acceptance of the listed company's first notice by the Exchange, the broker or agent then has a thirty day period within which to sell the securities involved. In other words, the underwriting price may be frozen for the thirty day period while the broker seeks out investor/clients with whom to place the securities.

Except as noted above, Listings Policy Statements Nos. 11 and 21 apply to brokered placements with the necessary contextual changes.

CHAPTER NINE

Incentive Stock Options

GENERAL REQUIREMENTS

The Exchange's incentive stock option policy regarding Venture Companies, the most junior of its listed companies, is currently one of the most complex and stringent of Canada's recognized stock exchanges. This policy must take into account volatile market prices, a relatively high turnover of directors of Venture Companies and the different interconnections between some of the listed companies and their management. Exchange Listings Policy Statement No. 1 sets out the requirements for the granting of incentive stock options in Venture Companies as well as Resource or Commercial/Industrial Companies. Initially, it should be pointed out that the types of individuals who qualify for stock options vary significantly between the categories of companies. A Venture Company is only permitted to grant stock options to its, or its subsidiary's, directors and employees. A Resource or Commercial/Industrial Company, in addition to granting stock options to directors and employees of it or its subsidiary, may grant options to persons who either perform services for the company on an ongoing basis or are expected to provide a service of value to the company. For example, consultants or professionals who provide services to the Resource or Commercial/Industrial Company would qualify for incentive stock options.

The incentive stock option policy has a number of general requirements which apply to both Venture Companies and Resource or Commercial/Industrial Companies. There are five general requirements: first, the aggregate number of shares which may be reserved for issuance for directors' stock option and employees' stock option or purchase plans is, in the aggregate, limited to 10% of the number of issued and outstanding shares of the company at the time the options are granted. In this connection, it must be noted that an optionee, or purchaser under such plans, must be a director or an employee of the listed company or its subsidiary at the time of the granting. This rule means that shares, and therefore a favourable exercise price, cannot be optioned as a reserve for future directors or employees. Furthermore, the Exchange, except in unusual circumstances, will not permit the 10% base amount to be calculated on shares to be issued in the future, as, for example, would be the case if a property acquisition was made at the time, or shortly after, a particular director joined the board of directors of a listed company. The actual number of issued and outstanding shares at the time the options are granted is the relevant number.

The second requirement is that the same individual is not permitted to be an optionee in respect of more than 5% of the issued and outstanding shares at the time the option is granted, whether or not it is granted as part of a stock option or pursuant to a share purchase plan.

The third rule relates to the number of listed companies in which the same person may hold an incentive stock option. An individual is not permitted to hold an incentive stock option in more than fifteen listed companies although the Exchange reserves the right to permit this limit to be exceeded in unusual circumstances on grounds established to its satisfaction.

The fourth rule is that optionees under incentive stock option agreements must be individuals. The Exchange will not accept an incentive stock option agreement for filing where the optionee is a legal entity other than an individual. This prohibition explicitly extends to management companies controlled by persons who would otherwise qualify as acceptable optionees.

The fifth rule is discretionary; it requires a listed company to distribute incentive stock options on an equitable basis. Factors which the Exchange will take into account are the number of employees and directors, the frequency of optionee turnover, the relative size of option allocations to new employees and directors, and the duties and qualifications of each optionee in relation to the optionee's position as a director or employee. The rationale for this general provision is that the Exchange wants to ensure that *bona fide* employees of listed companies are treated fairly in relation to their directors.

EXERCISE TERM AND SUBSEQUENT GRANT

The maximum exercise term of an incentive stock option agreement is, by virtue of Listings Policy Statement No. 1, limited to a maximum of ten years for Resource or Commercial/Industrial Companies and five years for Venture Companies. For most listed companies, therefore, the maximum exercise term will be five years. This exercise term compares very favourably to other Exchange-regulated exercise terms. Presumably, the reason the maximum exercise terms of incentive options are longer than those associated with most other types of Exchange-regulated exercise terms is that incentive options form a very significant part of the remuneration to directors and employees of Exchange-listed companies.

An incentive stock option must terminate prior to the expiry of its term where the optionee ceases to be a director or employee, as the case may be, of the listed company which granted the option. Listings Policy Statement No. 1 provides that an incentive stock option granted by a Venture Company must be exercised within 30 days after the optionee ceases to be a director or employee of the Venture Company. This restriction does not apply to a Resource or Commercial/Industrial Company although the matter of termination in the event the optionee ceases to be involved with the company should be dealt with in the stock option plan or agreement.

While the rule associated with the maximum exercise terms is straightforward, the question of subsequent grants in the case of Venture Companies is not, as there are three, interconnected sub-rules which operate together. The purpose of these three sub-rules is to reasonably restrict the number of times a Venture Company may grant incentive options to the same person. The thrust of these sub-rules is that an individual should only receive an incentive option from the same Venture Company a maximum of once every two years. Thus, if an option with an exercise term exceeding two years is exercised in the first or second year following its granting, a new incentive option may not be granted to that optionee until two years has elapsed from the original grant. An option with an exercise term of two or more years may be renegotiated as to the exercise price only one year after its granting. This assumes, of course, that the option has not been fully exercised. The option may be fully renegotiated providing at least two years have elapsed since the option was originally negotiated.

In the case of Resource or Commercial/Industrial Companies, a person may hold more than one incentive stock option in the same company at any given time, that is, a stock option need not be exercised or otherwise terminated before that person is granted another option.

EXERCISE PRICE

Under the provisions of Listings Policy Statement No. 1, the minimum exercise price applicable to both directors' and employees' incentive stock options must be fixed in relation to the per share trading price of the shares of the listed company granting the options. Subject to the effect of a special readjustment provision contained in Listings Policy Statement No. 1, which will be discussed presently, the exercise price of stock options granted by Venture Companies may not be less than the average closing price of the listed company's shares for the days that the company's shares traded within the ten trading day period preceding the day on which the options are granted and publicly announced by the listed company. In the case of Resource or Commercial/Industrial Companies, a discount from this average closing price may be used. The discounts are as follows:

Average	Discount
$1.00 or less	20%
$1.01 to $5.00	15%
Above $5.00	10%

In addition, the minimum exercise price of any incentive stock option granted by any type of listed company may not be less than $0.15.

The Exchange, which used to permit the using of discounts from the market price to determine the minimum exercise price of all incentive options, does not currently permit discounts to be used unless the listed company is a Resource or Commercial/Industrial Company. Furthermore, the exercise price selected must be at least equal to the exact average of the ten closing prices; if it is not, the Exchange will require an upward adjustment to the exercise price.

One of the more unique features of the Exchange's incentive stock option policy is its readjustment provision which applies only to options granted by Venture Companies. In mid-1984, the Exchange noticed a phenomenon of granting incentive options, shortly after public offerings, where the market price, and therefore the minimum exercise price of the incentive option, had fallen significantly below the public offering price. The Exchange, realizing this was an unfair practice because the investing public were paying more for their shares than the exercise price under the stock options, put a stop to the practice by developing, and enforcing, what has become known as the six month rule. This rule sets as a minimum exercise price, for each individual listed company, the actual public offering price per share for a six month period following a public distribution. The rule does not include private placement financings and does not appear to include shareholder rights offerings. The six month period commences at slightly different times depending on the type of public distribution. In the case of fixed price agency offerings, the offering day is the starting date. In the case of underwritings and open market distributions (best efforts agency offerings), the effective date of the SMF must be used. In the case of initial distributions, the full listing date must be used as the commencement date for the six month period. Where the public distribution was a unit offering, the average market price of the shares comprising the units, using Exchange Rules, must be used as the minimum exercise price. In the case of open market distributions, the average gross price paid for the listed company's shares sold must be used.

NEWS RELEASE

Listings Policy Statement No. 1 requires that a listed company which grants incentive stock options must publish a news release disclosing the incentive stock options on the day on which they were granted. Failure to do so probably will result in the Exchange refusing to accept the option agreements for filing if there has been an appreciation in the price of the listed company's shares. It is not uncommon to see news releases announcing options only disclosing the type of option (director or employee), the number of shares involved and the exercise price. The only requirements for disclosure in the news release are that any subsequent required approvals, such as shareholder and regulatory approvals, must be referred to as must the average closing price on which the exercise price is based.

The Exchange requires that all material changes must be publicly announced before options may be granted. The Exchange may require revision to the exercise price of a stock option if the price is based on the company's trading prices prior to adequate dissemination of a material announcement and the reflection of the announcement in the public market. In addition, incentive options may be granted before the listed company's announcement of what it considers a material transaction but prior to the filing of the stock options with the Exchange. In these cases, the Exchange will ascertain the specific knowledge of the listed company concerning either the negotiations leading up to the transaction or the transaction itself. If the listed company did have specific knowledge of the transaction at the time the options are granted, the Exchange will determine the minimum exercise price to be the closing price of the listed company's shares on the trading day after the announcement was made. In most cases, this represents a significant penalty.

OTHER REQUIREMENTS

Listings Policy Statement No. 1 contains a number of other requirements, most of which are more procedural than substantive. First, the Exchange sets out two, quite separate filing procedures associated with stock options which must be attended to within 30 days of the granting of the options. Under the first procedure, called the regular filing procedure, a true copy of the directors' resolution granting the option must be filed along with true copies of the various agreements. In addition, particulars of any existing directors' and employees' stock options held by any of the optionees must be given to the Exchange on a prescribed form (called a declaration of stock option position which is attached as Appendix 1 to Listings Policy Statement No. 1) as well as particulars of all proposed and outstanding stock options in the listed company and the requisite filing fee. Under the second procedure, called the certified filing procedure, a sample of the option agreement must be filed, together with the declaration of stock option position for each optionee, a declaration of certified filing (Appendix 2 to Listings Policy Statement No. 1) completed by a director or senior officer of the company, a summary form (Appendix 3 to Listings Policy Statement No. 1) disclosing, among other matters, all proposed and outstanding stock options of the company and the requisite filing fee. As with the certified filing procedures associated with private placements, the Exchange will automatically issue its acceptance letter where the certified filing procedure is used.

Exchange Listings Policy Statement No. 1 also sets out the contents of specific terms which must be included in each individual's option agreement. There must be a term that the agreement is non-assignable and non-transferable. There must be a term specifying the period, if any and not exceeding one year, after the death of the optionee, within which the heirs or administrators of the optionee's estate may exercise any portion of the outstanding option. In the case of options granted to insiders, as defined in s.1(1) of the *Act,* there must be a term requiring shareholder approval prior to its exercise and requiring shareholder approval in respect of any amendments to the agreement if the agreement itself was approved by shareholders or if the optionee is an insider at the time of amending. In the case of employee option agreements, the policy requires a representation that the optionee is an employee of the listed company or its subsidiary, granting the option. This policy also allows the Exchange to accept employee option agreements for individuals who are employees of a company which provides management services to the listed company. Moreover, the Exchange interprets the word employee quite loosely so as to permit individuals who would not ordinarily be thought of as employees to be optionees under employee option agreements.

Two final comments on incentive stock options are in order. If a listed company has been listed only for a short while, the Exchange generally will not permit it to grant incentive options until a stable, orderly market in its shares has been established. This length of time will vary for each individual company. A listed company must notify the Exchange, on a monthly basis, of all options exercised. This requirement is particularly important to the Exchange since these figures are transmitted to the Exchange staff members who are responsible for maintaining the capital base for the Exchange Index which is calculated on a capital weighted basis.

CHAPTER TEN

Share Consolidations

GENERAL

The topic of share consolidations, commonly called rollbacks or reverse splits, is usually one which does not arise in isolation. More often than not it arises in the context of an inactive, or shell company being reorganized (see Chapter 17). Usually the consolidation occurs concurrent to a change in management, to the issuance of shares for debt (see Chapter 11) and the issuance of additional principals' shares (see Chapter 14). Quite often, the listed company will be a dormant company as that term is defined in Securities Commission Local Policy Statement No. 3-35 (October 13, 1989). This gives rise to requirements in addition to those associated with share consolidations.

The Exchange's rules respecting share consolidations are contained in Listings Policy Statement No. 20. Prior to its original issuance in March, 1985, the only rules which the Exchange had in connection with share consolidations were unwritten rules to the effect that only a maximum ratio of 1:5 was permitted and that, concurrently with the consolidation, the listed company had to change its corporate name. With the publication of the original version of Listings Policy Statement No. 20, several additional requirements were imposed, some of which were dove-tailed to the Exchange's shares for debt policy (see Chapter 11).

Before discussing the specific requirements, it is worth noting that Listings Policy Statement No. 20 implicitly requires shareholder approval. Although not express, the Policy Statement speaks of the occurrence of certain events prior to the sending of an information circular and proxy material to shareholders. For a company incorporated under the *Company Act*, shareholder approval of a special resolution is required to consolidate any of its shares. For the most part, most of the statutory corporate requirements of other jurisdictions require prior shareholder approval, in one form or another, to effect a share consolidation. These requirements will have to be borne in mind when undertaking a share consolidation.

Another circumstance which sometimes exists at the time of a consolidation is that the listed company may have warrants or options outstanding. These warrants may be in the form of agents' warrants issued in connection with an Exchange offering, publicly traded warrants issued by the listed company in a unit offering, or warrants granted as partial consideration for a private placement. The options referred to may be underwriter's options, incentive stock options, or options granted in connection with a private placement of the listed company's securities. Whether the constating documents creating these various calls on the listed company speak to the situation or not, the Exchange will assume and require the exercise price and call amount of the option or warrant to be changed in accordance with the consolidation ratio, such changes to be effected concurrent with the consolidation. A share consolidation does not affect the exercise period of the option or warrant, that is, the length of the time within which the call must be exercised. For example, assume that there is an outstanding option representing a call on 200,000 shares, exercisable at $0.20 per share. Assume further that the listed company consolidates its authorized and issued capital on a 1:5 basis. Given the consolidation, the total number of the call amount of the incentive stock option would be reduced to 40,000, with an exercise price of $1.00 per share. By way of another example, assume that a listed company has 400,000 publicly traded share purchase warrants. Assume that these warrants are exercisable on a 2:1 requirement basis (i.e. two warrants are required to purchase a further share) at $0.20 per share. If the same 1:5 share consolidation occurs, then ten such warrants, as well as $1.00, will be required to purchase one consolidated share. The Exchange, while it does not have a written policy on the matter, requires the exercise price of outstanding calls, and the number of shares on which there is a call, to be changed when the capital alteration occurs. It is important to remember that where there are listed warrants trading through the facilities of the Exchange, the listed company should, on the effective date of the share consolidation, issue a news release setting forth the new exercise price, otherwise a disorderly market in the warrants may develop.

SPECIFIC REQUIREMENTS

There are six specific requirements which the Exchange has enacted, all of which are contained in Listings Policy Statement No. 20. The first requirement is that the corporate name of the listed company must be changed as part of the consolidation process. The new name must be different enough when compared to the listed company's previous name so as to ensure that there will be no confusion on the part of the investing public insofar as share certificates representing pre-consolidated and post-consolidated shares are concerned. Usually, this aspect of the Exchange requirement is not problematical since a completely new and different name is selected to describe a new corporate undertaking or a new control group. Sometimes, however, the management and undertaking of the listed company are not changed and management want to keep a similar name and make as minor a change as possible. As a minimum, the Exchange will require a prefix to the main part of the name; a change to the subordinate or adjectival part of the name will not be sufficient. For example, if the name of the listed company was Acme Resources Ltd., the name Acme Industries Corporation likely will not be acceptable. The prefix words New, Consolidated, or International however, will be acceptable.

The second requirement is that the listed company must issue a news release disclosing the proposed consolidation no later than the time the company sends its information circular and proxy material to its shareholders. It should be noted that this particular Policy Statement speaks only of the latest point when the news release may be issued. As with all capital alterations, a proposed share consolidation is considered by the Exchange to represent a material change in the affairs of a listed company and, accordingly, a news release should be issued, at the latest, immediately after the listed company's board of directors decides to put the question of the share consolidation to the company's shareholders.

Not only does the Listings Policy Statement require the timely issuance of a news release, it also sets out the minimum disclosure requirements associated with these types of news releases. It goes without saying that the news release would also have to comply with the terms of the Exchange timely disclosure policy and the timely disclosure provisions contained in s.67 of the *Securities Act* (see Chapter 18). Seven disclosure matters are prescribed, the first of which is that the proposed consolidation ratio must be disclosed. The number of currently outstanding shares, as well as the number outstanding after the consolidation, must also be disclosed. The reason, or reasons, for the consolidation must be spelled out and the date of the shareholders meeting must be disclosed. The fact that the consolidation is subject to both shareholder and Exchange approval also must be included in the same news release. Finally, and the need for the following opinion will be discussed presently, if a special opinion of a Member is required, that fact will have to be disclosed with the name of the brokerage firm providing that opinion.

The third requirement is two-fold. If the listed company is an inactive listed company as that term is defined in Listings Policy Statement No. 17 (see Chapter 17) then the Exchange will not approve a share consolidation unless the listed company is undergoing a reorganization as that term is defined in the same Listings Policy Statement. After the share consolidation has been completed, the listed company must be in full compliance with the minimum listing standards commensurate with its listing category. The

Exchange does not wish to see shell companies, or near shell companies, reorganized in a haphazard and disorganized fashion. Rather, the Exchange wants to see its listed companies reorganized in such a way as to ensure, more or less, a benefit to its shareholders; the Exchange wants to foster the prospect of a new, reorganized publicly traded company as opposed to one involved in a slow, disorganized metamorphosis.

The fourth requirement, coupled with the effect of the fifth requirement, has turned out to be moderately stringent. The Exchange will not approve a share consolidation which has the effect of reducing the issued capital of the listed company to less than 1,000,000 shares. This particular number excludes any shares issued as principals' or escrow shares and any other shares which are proposed to be issued as part of a subsequent, but related, private placement or Exchange offering. The 1,000,000 threshold number does include any post-consolidated shares issued to settle debt. As an example, assume a listed company has 3,750,000 shares issued and outstanding and proposes to issue 250,000 post-consolidated shares by way of debt settlement immediately after the share consolidation. The maximum consolidation ratio which the Exchange would accept given its policy requirements, everything else equal, would be 1:5 since the consolidation will originally yield 750,000 and the addition of the 250,000 shares to this number will yield 1,000,000. This distinction is made because the Exchange has tried favourably to minimize the dilution effect of consolidation on existing shareholders where the debt of the listed company is relatively small.

The fifth requirement is that the Exchange will not accept a share consolidation with a ratio of greater than 1:5 unless the number of pre-consolidated issued and outstanding shares exceeds 10,000,000. If the number of issued and outstanding shares exceeds 10,000,000, then a greater than 1:5 share consolidation ratio may be used, subject to the 1,000,000 share minimum threshold discussed above. If the number of pre-consolidated issued and outstanding shares of the listed company is less than 10,000,000 then a consolidation ratio greater than 1:5 may be used, subject to the same 1,000,000 share minimum discussed above, if and only if a Member brokerage firm prepared to file with the Exchange its opinion that such a consolidation is a necessary and advisable part of a reorganization of the listed company's affairs. This brokerage firm must be a Member which is proposing to act as the listed company's agent or underwriter in an Exchange offering subsequent to the consolidation. Implicit, then, in this requirement is the notion that a public financing by an Exchange offering will be required where the ratio is greater than 1:5 unless the pre-consolidated number of outstanding shares exceeds 10,000,000.

The sixth, and final requirement is that the listed company must seek the Exchange's approval for the share consolidation, and the proposed change of name, not later than the time at which the shareholders' meeting is held. This is to ensure an expeditious filing. The Exchange also prohibits the filing of the shareholders' resolutions respecting the consolidation and change of corporate name with the Registrar of Companies, or similar corporate regulatory agency, until the Exchange has approved both. Accordingly, the listing and posting of the new shares and the filing with the Registrar of Companies will have to be coordinated to occur on the same day.

CHAPTER ELEVEN

Share For Debt

GENERAL

The Exchange's rules dealing with a listed company proposing to settle debt by way of the issuance of its common shares from treasury are covered in Listings Policy Statement No. 8. Usually the issue of debt settlements by issuing shares arises in connection with a reorganization as that term is defined in Listings Policy Statement No. 17 (see Chapter 17). Policy Statement No. 8 has been revised since it was first published to regulate more stringently the issuance of shares for debt in situations where extremely large amounts of shares were being issued by a few listed companies as part of a particular type of corporate reorganization. The preamble to the subject Policy Statement indicates that it applies in situations where the listed company is unable, or in certain circumstances unwilling, to make payment in cash of trade or other accounts payable of the listed company.

Notwithstanding the wording of the preamble, the Exchange generally does not permit a listed company to pay debts by treasury share issuances as long as the listed company has cash funds to pay for those debts. The argument that the listed company is trying to conserve cash will not, except in the rarest of cases, be accepted by the Exchange. In practice then, the Exchange has written out of the Policy Statement the words "or in certain circumstances unwilling".

There are five general rules governing debt settlements, the first of which is that the listed company must have no funds, or immediate source of funds to pay the debts in question, or that funds on hand have been otherwise committed. This must be evident from the listed company's financial statements, and must be established to the satisfaction of the Exchange.

The second rule is that the Exchange will require the listed company's shareholders to approve the issuance of shares where it may result in an effective change of control of the listed company. While Listings Policy Statement No. 8 does not specifically provide a test for what constitutes an effective change in control, the Exchange uses the test embodied in Listings

Policy Statement No. 11, the Exchange's Policy Statement dealing with private placements (see Chapter 8). That is, shareholder approval will be required where the issuance, if the number of shares to be issued to one creditor, or group of creditors who intend to vote their shares as a group, is equal to or greater than 20% of the number of the company's shares outstanding after giving effect to the issuance of the shares to be issued to settle the debt, or debts, as the case may be. Similarly, if the shares to be issued may create a control block, shareholder approval will be required.

The third rule deals with hold periods, which are separate and apart from any hold periods and resale restrictions which may be imposed under the *Securities Act*. In the case of issuances of shares to insiders of the listed company, the Exchange may impose a hold period of up to twelve months from the date on which the debt was incurred. This provision is seldom applied, and then usually only in cases where the shares for debt method was clearly used in the stead of a private placement to avoid the hold period associated with a private placement. In the case of arm's length creditors, a hold period will not be imposed by the Exchange unless a pattern of these types of settlements to a particular creditor has been established. In this situation, the Exchange views the transaction as being one more closely associated with a private placement transaction, and thus will impose a twelve month hold period.

The deemed price at which the shares may be issued forms the subject of the fourth rule. The minimum deemed price may not be less than the average market price (the average closing price) of the company's shares over the two week period immediately preceding the day on which the settlement agreement is reached and, in any event, may not be less than $0.15 per share. However, if the shares are required to be held for a period of one year, then the shares may be issued at a discount to the average price. In this case, the maximum discount schedule permitted for private placement financings as set out in Exchange Listings Policy Statement No. 11 may be used (see Chapter 8).

The final rule is probably the most important and applies only to Venture Companies. It requires the effect of the debt conversion to result in the company being in a positive working capital position or in one that will otherwise permit the listed company to secure financing to alleviate a negative working capital position. In other words, the Exchange will not permit a piece-meal, haphazard approach to be taken by listed companies.

DEBT RESTRUCTURING PLANS

In early 1985, the Exchange observed a new phenomenon: a small number of listed companies with very large debts were being reorganized by the settlement of debts in a situation where the debts were being purchased, or consolidated, by one individual. The result of the transactions was that one individual owned an unusually large percentage of the outstanding voting shares of the listed company. The number of shares being issued was such that three and four times the pre-settlement outstanding share capital were being issued. Accordingly, in March 1985, the Exchange issued an Addendum to Listings Policy Statement No. 8. (It also issued Listings Policy Statement No. 20, representing the Exchange's share consolidation policy.) The original Addendum was revised, and a new one issued on July 4, 1985; it was further revised in August, 1985 and is now contained in Listings Policy Statement No. 8. As noted, the Addendum was created to deal with specific policy issues arising out of what the Exchange called debt restructuring plans. Notwithstanding this, the Addendum has now been merged with the Policy Statement itself and is now applicable to any debt settlement.

The first two rules apply only to Venture Companies and set a maximum limit on the number of shares which may be issued under a debt settlement scheme. The maximum number of shares is limited to the lesser of 1,000,000 shares, whether pre-consolidation or post-consolidation shares, or 100% of the number of the company's existing issued and outstanding shares excluding any principals' or escrow shares which are proposed to be issued, and any other shares which are proposed to be issued as part of a subsequent private placement or public financing. While not expressly stated, the 100% limit applies to both the pre-consolidated issued share capital and the post-consolidated share capital.

The third special rule associated with debt restructuring plans is a complicated minimum deemed pricing rule which comes into play if, and only if, there is a share consolidation involved in the plan. In these cases, the minimum deemed price of any shares being issued as part of the debt settlement must be calculated by multiplying the number of unconsolidated shares required to be exchanged for one consolidated share by the greater of $0.15 or the prevailing market price. For example, if a 1:5 share consolidation is proposed as part of the reorganization, then the minimum deemed issuance price which will have to be used to determine the maximum allowable number of shares to be issued will be the greater of $0.75 or five times the prevailing market price of the company's shares.

As can be seen, the combined effect of these rules, and the Exchange's share consolidation rules (see Chapter 10) operate to create a relatively strict mechanism, all of which are designed to force the management of an inactive listed company to treat the listed company's shareholders fairly. The other side of the same coin, of course, is that if the Exchange's rules are viewed as being too strict in a given situation, then the company, and more importantly its public shareholders, may be abandoned.

The last special rule associated with debt restructuring plans is a general one. It provides that the Exchange must refuse an application to issue shares by way of debt settlement if it is satisfied that the plan is prejudicial to the public interest. The specific situation which the Exchange was addressing with this clause was that in which a third party was proposing to purchase the shares issued for a significant debt as part of a restructuring plan. The Exchange will reject a plan where a third party purchases, or agrees to purchase, shares issued for pre-existing debt for a lesser amount than the debt settled, that is, the amount the listed company paid to its creditors under the initial debt settlement. Where the purchase arrangement is one involving payments over time, then the discounted value of those payments will have to be used in assessing the calculation. The reason for this particular prohibition is that the Exchange is of the view that the third party should not reap a profit from the hands of the company's *bona fide* creditors.

CHAPTER TWELVE

Management Remuneration, Transactions with Insiders and with Brokers

GENERAL

The three topics which are covered in this chapter have a common theme: all relate to consideration being paid by a listed company to two special groups, insiders and brokers. This is an area where securities regulators have traditionally been expected to have strict rules, since the relationship between the listed company and both of these groups has been considered non-arm's length, or at least a relationship involving dealings with non-public members. Not surprisingly then, the Exchange has two separate Listings Policy Statements dealing with management remuneration and transactions with insiders and two Exchange Rules dealing with transactions between listed companies and brokers.

MANAGEMENT REMUNERATION

The topic of management remuneration forms the subject of Listings Policy Statement No. 7. First published as a policy statement in 1983, it provides that the management of a listed company may be paid when the listed company is solvent and is conducting its affairs to reach its corporate objectives. The Policy Statement goes on to provide that the maximum aggregate fees which may be paid to the management of Venture Companies which have no positive cash flow or immediate source of funds, excluding any funds available from public financings, is $2,500.00 per month. It also provides that these limits may be varied depending upon the stage of development of the company, the qualifications of management and the particular type of services they provide. Regarding the latter and particularly in the case of non-resource companies, the Exchange generally recognizes that these minimum limits are relatively low, and is therefore amenable to permitting higher monthly amounts to be paid so long as the listed company has the cash funds to make these payments; the individual in question devotes his entire time to the affairs of the company; the proposed salary level is not inconsistent with general industry standards; and the proposed salary is generally consistent with the person's previous salary level.

It should be noted that this particular Policy Statement deals only with management remuneration. It does not deal with fees paid to management companies providing administrative services to listed companies where the management companies are controlled by the insiders of the listed company. In this latter case, as long as the fees are consistent with industry standards and the listed company is being competently serviced, there should be no objection by the Exchange to the making of these payments. In both of the above-noted cases, the prior approval of the Exchange is required since both involve transactions between the listed company and an insider. An agreement setting out the responsibilities and specific services to be provided must be filed for acceptance by the Exchange.

TRANSACTIONS WITH INSIDERS

While the Exchange is of the view that it should not be in the boardroom of listed companies, it is also of the view that asset acquisition transactions involving a listed company and its insiders must be regulated in the public interest. This regulation is found in Listings Policy Statement No. 12. The classes of entities that the Exchange regulates by this particular Policy Statement does not include all insiders as that term is defined in s.1(1) of the *Securities Act*. For the purposes of this policy, the term insider only includes directors, senior officers, promoters and their associates, as defined in the *Act*. It should be noted that the term promoter is defined in a classical sense by the *Act*, and that the term associates includes companies in which an insider has more than a 10% voting interest as well as relatives who share the same home as that occupied by the insider. Specifically, the definition does not include insiders who are insiders of the listed company only by virtue of their shareholdings in the listed company; 10% shareholders, and even control persons, are not included in the definition. The reason for this exclusion is that the Exchange did not want to go beyond the fiduciary duty standards established by common law over the years. In other words, the Exchange did not want to, in essence, prescribe a fiduciary duty in the absence of one created in law.

It should be noted that Listings Policy Statement No. 12 only deals with acquisitions of an asset by a listed company, not dispositions of assets made by it to insiders. In regard to dispositions of corporate assets to insiders, the

Exchange does not have a published policy. The unwritten policy is that these transactions must be carried out in such a way as to ensure that the listed company receives at least fair market value for the asset. The Exchange will also require the listed company's shareholders to approve the disposition.

The Policy Statement divides transactions into two types, those where the insider has held the asset for more than one year and those where the asset has been owned for less than one year. Generally speaking, the policy structure is designed to prevent profitable flip transactions, which in most cases would be a clear breach of a director's or senior officer's fiduciary duties owed to the listed company.

In cases where the asset has been owned for more than one year, the Exchange will only accept the acquisition agreement for filing if three conditions are met. First, the insider must have increased the value of the asset from the time he acquired it due to his own efforts. That rule would not be satisfied, for example, in a situation where the value of certain mining claims had increased due to a general increase in mining activity in the area or due to significant mineral discoveries close by. This particular rule implicitly permits an insider to acquire an asset, to do some development work on it, and then sell it to the listed company at a time when some of the risk associated initially with the asset has been reduced.

The second rule under these circumstances is that the proposed consideration must be fair and reasonable. It also must comply with any general requirements which the Exchange applies to the same type of transaction where it does not involve an insider.

The third rule is that the listed company's shareholders must approve the transaction. In this regard, there is no prohibition against the involved insider voting shares which may be owned by the insider. It should also be observed that the Policy Statement does not prescribe a special resolution. In cases of this sort, the type of shareholders' resolution will only depend on the general rules of corporate law.

The second area covered by Listings Policy Statement No. 12 relates to situations where the asset being acquired by the listed company has not been owned by the insider for more than one year. In this case, the very stringent regulations covering the transaction are threefold. The first two are identical to the first and third requirements discussed above, namely, the value of the asset must have been increased over its initial value due to the efforts of the insider and the transaction must be approved by the company's shareholders. The third rule in this situation stipulates a maximum consideration which may be paid to the insider by the listed company in addition to the insider's out-of-pocket expenses related to acquiring and enhancing the asset. In the case of natural resource assets, the maximum consideration is limited to a fair and reasonable net profits interest after the commencement of commercial production. In the case of non-natural resource assets, the maximum consideration is limited to a fair and reasonable net profits interest. In both cases, the net profits interest may not exceed more than 5% of the interest acquired by the listed company. These provisions are relatively prohibitive and consequently it is not surprising to learn that there are very few assets acquired by listed companies from their insiders. This was, and remains, the desired result of this particular aspect of the Exchange's policy.

There are two circumstances where the Exchange will relax the net profits interest requirements and permit the payment of consideration prior to the time otherwise permitted under those rules. These two circumstances are, first, where the insider acquired the asset prior to the time he became an insider of the listed company and, second, when, at the time the insider acquired the asset, the listed company did not have the financial resources to acquire the asset.

The final observation on this area relates, not to Exchange regulations, but to the corporate law applicable to all transactions (not just asset acquisitions) between a company and parties which owe that company fiduciary duties. While such transactions may comply with the minimum requirements set forth by the Exchange, it must be borne in mind that the requirements of the *Company Act* and the common law must also be satisfied. If these latter requirements are not complied with, the transaction may be voided by a court of competent jurisdiction.

TRANSACTIONS WITH BROKERS

Transactions between listed companies and brokers have always been regulated for the same reason that insider transactions are regulated: both inherently involve potential conflicts of interest. As far back as 1975 when the Superintendent of Brokers issued a Notice (September 11, 1975), attention was drawn to the fact that securities salesmen may have unresolvable conflicts of interest if they sat on the board of directors, or were officers, of listed companies. The basic conflict would be between the salesman's duty to his clients and the salesman's corporate duties owed to the listed company. This particular concern had been previously recognized in 1971 and embodied in National Policy Statement No. 18. In *In the Matter of John D. Gunther*, Corporate and Financial Services Commission (May 27, 1976), the Commission pointed out the difficult position that a securities salesman may find himself in if he became appraised of material information that was not available to the public. As a director, he would be precluded from divulging that information by virtue of the provisions of the *Securities Act* and, at the same time, would be placed in an impossible situation vis-a-vis his clients. By not telling them the information, he may not be servicing them adequately and may, in fact, be negligent. Accordingly, in the mid-1970's, the Exchange adopted the rule now embodied in Exchange Rule F.2.25 (see Chapter 2). Based on the same rationale, it subsequently adopted rules governing transactions between salesmen and companies which had their securities listed for trading on the Exchange. These rules are embodied in Exchange Rules F.2.26 and 2.27.

Exchange Rule F.2.26 prohibits any securities salesman, and any other employee of a brokerage firm, whether they are residents of British Columbia and whether they are under the jurisdiction of the Exchange, from selling, or being part of a group selling, assets to any listed company without the prior approval of the Exchange. Moreover, such persons may not be compensated, directly or indirectly, for acting as a finder or agent for such transactions unless the prior approval of the Exchange is obtained (see Chapter 15). As a practical matter, this approval is never given. The Exchange regards this rule as being so important that such applications are ruled upon by the Board of Governors, not the Exchange Listing Committee. In recent years, the Board of Governors has not approved any such transactions, and most are usually withdrawn.

Exchange Rule F.2.27 contains a similar prohibition against listed companies selling assets to securities salesmen and other employees of brokerage firms.

Comments are in order on these two rules. First, neither Rule applies to a director, officer or a partner of a brokerage firm. The rationale of the Exchange is that those persons usually do not have the same client contact that securities salesmen do. Whether this is a valid rationale may be debatable. Second, both Rules prohibit, in the absence of prior Exchange approval, direct or indirect payments. This is generally not interpreted to prohibit, for example, the payment of a finder's fee to a brokerage firm which, in turn, splits that fee with a securities salesman pursuant to a previously agreed upon arrangement. The indirect aspects of the Rules are generally interpreted to refer to disguised and undisclosed payments to securities salesmen. Third, both Rules apply, by virtue of Exchange Rule F.2.25.2, to securities salesmen and brokerage firm employees wherever they may reside and whether the brokerage firm is otherwise under the membership jurisdiction of the Exchange or not. In *In the Matter of Mariah Resources Ltd.*, Corporate and Financial Services Commission (December 21, 1984), the Exchange refused to conditionally list a company going public in British Columbia where an optionor of one of the company's natural resource properties was a stock salesman employed by a brokerage firm located in Portland, Oregon. At that time, the Exchange Rule dealing with acquisitions from securities salesmen (called registered representatives) did not include a reference to salesman wherever they be resident. On appeal, the Commission upheld the ruling of the Exchange by indicating that the policy behind the Rule was not, in substance, an attempt by the Exchange at regulating the conduct of foreign brokerage firms but was rather, in pith and substance, a listing rule which the Exchange could quite properly adopt and enforce in the public interest.

CHAPTER THIRTEEN

Listed Companies Purchasing Shares

GENERAL

The Exchange's written regulation governing situations where a listed company proposes to acquire shares, and presumably other securities such as warrants, of another listed company is to be found in Listings Policy Statements No. 3 and No. 4. The former Listings Policy Statement deals with arm's length purchases; the latter covers purchases not considered by the Exchange to be at arm's length. These two areas of regulation are the subject of this Chapter.

Before examining these two areas, it should be noted that each of these Listings Policy Statements have been published in revised form. In fact, there have been numerous versions of both Policy Statements. The most significant changes incorporated into the current versions were the modifications made in December, 1984 in which development companies, now categorized by the Exchange as Venture Companies, were precluded from making either type of purchase and the modifications made in March, 1984 to the non-arm's length Policy Statement, No. 4, deleting a two-day advance news release requirement and adding a one-year listing requirement. It should be observed that both Listings Policy Statements deal with primary and secondary purchases, that is purchases made of a company's treasury securities as well as previously issued securities. Venture Companies are not permitted to make either of these types of purchases, shares acquired in non-arm's length purchases must be held for one year and any purchases may only be made from surplus funds.

It should be noted also that neither these two Listings Policy Statements, nor any other Listings Policy Statement, deal with situations where a listed company wishes to purchase its own shares. These types of purchases, which are also regulated by ss.260 and 261 of the *Company Act* and, in all likelihood, by the Articles of the listed company itself, are now called issuer bids, the terminology used in the *Securities Act* to describe the purchase by a listed company by way of an offer to acquire or redeem any of its own securities other than debt securities which are not convertible into equity securities. Prior to February 1, 1987, the date on which the new *Act* came into force, the Exchange had an unwritten policy of applying the provisions of Listings Policy Statement No. 4 to issuer bids. In other words, if a listed company wished to purchase or otherwise redeem any of its listed securities, its application would be accepted so long as it complied with, and otherwise met the terms of, Listings Policy Statement No. 4. This also had been the Exchange's practice between February 1, 1987 and December 28, 1987 since the Exchange's take-over bid rule, Exchange Rule B.4.00, did not contain formal requirements for issuer bids. However, on December 29, 1987, the Exchange adopted as interim guidelines the issuer bid rules of the Toronto Stock Exchange or, if so elected by the listed company, the rules of the Montreal Exchange. On March 10, 1988, the Exchange published a revised Rule B.4.00 and also published a new Listings Policy Statement, No. 23 entitled *Stock Exchange Take-Over Bids and Issuer Bids*. These regulations now make the Exchange's regulation of take-over bids and issuer bids substantially uniform with the regulations adopted by the Toronto Stock, and Montreal, Exchanges. Some of these interim guidelines were further revised, on a temporary basis, on September 1, 1989. Accordingly, Listings Policy Statements Nos. 3 and 4 as well as the take-over bid and issuer bid provisions of the above-noted regulations will have to be referred to when one is dealing with take-over bids and issuer bids. This chapter deals only with Listings Policy Statements Nos. 3 and 4.

ARM'S LENGTH PURCHASES

A listed company which is either a Resource or Commercial/Industrial Company and which proposes to acquire shares of another listed company where there are no common insiders need concern itself only with the provisions of Listings Policy Statement No. 3. As a practical matter, the Exchange uses the definition of "insider" contained in s.1(1) of the *Securities Act* to demark the boundary between the two Policy Statements. Venture Companies are not permitted by the Exchange to make arm's length purchases. Exempt companies need not comply with the specific terms of the Policy Statement. Nevertheless, exempt companies would have to comply with the Exchange's corporate disclosure Listings Policy Statement No. 10 if the purchases represent a material change in its business or affairs and would, in any event, have to comply with the take-over bid provisions contained in Part 11 of the *Act*.

The first requirement of the Policy Statement is that the company must have been listed on the Exchange for more than one year. The time a company may have been conditionally listed cannot be counted for the purposes of this calculation. However, periods of suspensions, unless imposed for extraordinary reasons, are counted by the Exchange. In short, the Exchange uses a calendar basis for calculating the one year period. The second requirement is that only surplus funds of the listed company may be used to make such purchases. Surplus funds for this purpose are defined as those corporate funds derived from option or warrant exercise, unallocated working capital or cash flow. Moreover, the listed company must have enough surplus funds left over after the purchase program has been concluded to cover normal operating expenses for a period of one year.

The maximum permitted to be expended by a listed company by the provisions of Listings Policy Statement No. 3 in the absence of prior Exchange approval is $250,000.00. If a listed company proposes to expend more than $250,000.00 on an arm's length purchase program, then the prior approval of the Exchange will be required. In these cases, there must be an exceptional reason for the purchase. For example, if the target company owns a resource property adjacent to that owned by the applicant, then the application should be successful. Other circumstances which the Exchange would look on favourably are pre-amalgamation purchases, purchases made in contemplation of a formal take-over bid and situations where, for one reason or another, the investment opportunity is extremely favourable to the applicant company.

Listed companies which have completed an arm's length purchase program are required to give the Exchange notice of the transactions within five days of completing the purchases. Moreover, notice must be given to the Exchange five days after all sales of shares previously purchased in an arm's length program have been made. Public disclosure is not referred to in the Policy Statement, however, it must be remembered that if the purchases, or sales, constitute a material change in the listed company's affairs, then there must be compliance with the Exchange's corporate disclosure policy. Additionally, if applicable provisions of the *Act* are triggered, (such as the insider reporting requirements set out in s.70(2) or the special 10% special reporting required by s.93) then compliance will also have to be made with those provisions.

NON-ARM'S LENGTH PURCHASES

Venture Companies are not permitted by the Exchange to make non-arm's length purchases of another listed company's securities. A Resource or Commercial/Industrial Company which proposes to acquire shares of another listed company and where there is a common insider, must comply with the requirements of Listings Policy Statement No. 4. The provisions of this particular Policy Statement require prior Exchange approval, except for exempt companies before a purchase program may commence. This prior approval requirement exists so that the Exchange can be satisfied that the purpose of the program is not objectionable and that the Exchange is in a position to monitor such purchases. Exchange approval will not be given where the target company is about to conduct, or is in the process of conducting, an Exchange offering. Similarly, where the Exchange concludes that the primary purpose of the purchase program is to increase demand for the target company's shares, and therefore its price per share, its approval will not be given.

The general requirements associated with non-arm's length purchases are, with some additions, similar to those associated with arm's length purchases. As before, only surplus funds, as defined above, may be used and the company must, after having expended the purchase funds, have sufficient financial resources to cover one year of normal operating expenses. Similarly, the applicant company's shares must have been, at the time of the application to the Exchange, fully listed on the Exchange for more than a one year period. As opposed to the Policy Statement dealing with arm's length purchases, there is no minimum listing period requirement associated with the target company. There is one additional requirement, and that is that any shares purchased must be held for a minimum 12 month period. This is to ensure that the purchases are being made as an investment. The shares may be disposed of prior to the expiry of the one year period if the Exchange approves of such dispositions. By necessary implication, the Exchange will only consent in unusual circumstances. It will reluctantly approve of dispositions where the listed company has become low in cash reserves and wishes to improve its cash position. The Exchange will ordinarily approve a disposition if the listed company requires cash, or simply wishes to trade the shares, in connection with an acquisition of an asset of unusual merit. The Exchange will also approve dispositions within the one year period where the shares have become the subject of a take-over bid. An application based on the argument that now is a good time to sell, will not be successful.

Since prior Exchange approval is required before the purchase program commences, a filing with the Exchange is necessary. The documentation requirements are set forth in the Listings Policy Statement. First, there must be a declaration, which need not be sworn under oath, signed by all the directors of the company declaring that the cash to be used to purchase the target company's shares are surplus funds. Second, there must be written reasons given demonstrating the investment merit of the proposed purchases to the listed company making the application. The target company must have significant mineral reserves, cash flow or net assets to justify the investment. While the Listings Policy Statement seems to imply otherwise, the Exchange will occasionally accept other reasons, one of which would be that the applicant company has a resource property or asset of merit and the target company has an adjacent resource property or a complimentary, or competing, asset. Third, the directors' resolution approving the proposed purchase of the target company's shares must be filed. The fourth document which must be filed is a declaration signed by all directors and other insiders who exercise control over the affairs of the applicant company to the effect that they, as a group, will not buy or sell shares of the target company during the period when the applicant company commences purchasing shares to the time it issues the news release announcing the termination and results of the purchase program. This trading ban, monitored by reviewing the insider reports of the persons affected, forms part of this particular Listings Policy Statement to ensure that the applicant company is not competing with its own insiders in buying shares of the target company and is not, insofar as the selling ban is concerned, bailing out its own insiders from their share positions in the target company. This particular ban is not to be found in the Exchange's arm's length Listings Policy Statement. That notwithstanding, the Exchange would not look favourably upon insiders of the applicant company who bought or sold to the applicant company, shares of the target company, even on an arm's length basis.

Aside from the fee established by the Exchange for the filing, the only other document comprising the filing is a draft news release. This news release, notwithstanding the disclaimer that the contents are not approved by the Exchange, is vetted by the Exchange to ensure that the information prescribed by the subject Listings Policy Statement is set out in the release. The merits and risks of the investment must be disclosed, the maximum number of shares of the target company to be purchased and the duration of the purchase program must be set forth, the maximum funds to be expended by the applicant company and the percentage of those funds to surplus funds must be described, and any interest which the directors and other insiders of the applicant company may have in the shares and management of the target company must be disclosed. In addition, a summary of the material current activities and plans of both companies must be set forth in the news release.

The final requirement under the Listings Policy Statement associated with these types of non-arm's length purchases is that, on completion of the purchase program, the applicant company must issue a news release stating not only the total cost of the program but the actual number of shares purchased.

CHAPTER FOURTEEN

Escrow Shares

SUBSEQUENT ISSUANCES OF PRINCIPALS' SHARES

A. General

As discussed in Chapter 2, when a company goes public, that is, when it conducts its initial public offering, Securities Commission Local Policy Statement No. 3-07 (February 6, 1987) permits the prior issuance of up to 750,000 principals' shares. The minimum price per share for these principals' shares is $0.01, thus, these shares are often referred to as penny stock. These shares are only issuable to principals: directors, senior officers or promoters, or their holding companies (in which they have a greater than 50% interest), of the company going public.

At the present time, while the Securities Commission has recommended a new categorization of escrow shares, designated as principals' shares for both resource and non-resource companies (see Chapter 2), it is not known whether the Exchange will introduce a definitive policy dealing with the issuance of additional escrow, or principals' shares, for non-resource companies. Accordingly, the present discussion is limited to dealing with the issuance of additional principals' shares by resource and non-resource companies.

It is not unusual for a company which has gone public to be unsuccessful in its first business venture. After it has expended its initial funds, represented by the cash proceeds from the sale of its seed capital and initial public offering, a listed company may become what the securities regulators call dormant or inactive and what others call a shell company. However it is defined,the company usually has only one asset, which is not reflected on its balance sheet because it is the company's listing on the Exchange. In 1984, the Exchange observed that, everything else equal, the number of new companies going public was far in excess of those inactive listed companies which were being reorganized and subsequently financed, much to the detriment of these latter companies' shareholders. Accordingly, the Special Committee as part of its study on basic securities regulatory trends, developed the predecessor policy to what is now Listings Policy

Statement No. 17 to encourage the reactivation of shell companies, called inactive companies by the Special Committee. The subsequent issuance of principals' shares, called additional principals' shares in the Listings Policy Statement, is permitted to facilitate the reactivation and reorganization of the listed company so that its principals, mainly its directors, can obtain a measure of voting control as an incentive to develop the company. Implicit in this regulatory scheme is the premise that there are either little or no existing principals' shares outstanding or that their number will be substantially reduced as a result of a share consolidation undertaken as part of the reorganization.

It should be noted at this juncture that there is a difference made by the Exchange between an inactive company which is not trading (has its shares suspended from trading) and one which may otherwise be inactive but which continues to have its securities listed, posted and called for trading on the Exchange. In the former case, the inactive company is not considered eligible by the Listings Policy Statement to issue additional principals' shares. Moreover, and as will be discussed in Chapter 17, this type of inactive company will be required, if it undertakes a reorganization, to achieve full compliance with all of the Exchange's initial listing requirements. In the case of inactive trading companies, the reorganization must achieve compliance with certain relaxed initial listing standards.

The application of the Listings Policy Statement turns on two basic elements. First, there must be a reorganization; second, the listed company being reorganized must fall into an exacting definition of an inactive company. For the purposes of the Listings Policy Statement, an inactive listed company is one which, firstly, has not expended more than $50,000.00 on account of exploration or development expenditures if it is a resource company or $100,000.00 on expenditures directly related to the development of its assets if it is a non-resource company during the year period prior to its reorganization. Secondly, the listed company cannot have issued any of its securities for cash by a distribution to the public, including a rights offering, in that one year period if it is a resource company or the previous 18 months if it is a non-resource company.

Private placements may have been conducted during the above-noted periods and similarly, share for debt settlement arrangements may have been concluded without disqualifying the company from being an inactive one for the purposes of the definition.

Thirdly, the listed company cannot have received any significant revenue during the previous six months if it is a resource company and one year if it is a non-resource company and fourthly, it cannot have working capital to cover more than six months of normal operating expenses if it is a resource company and one year if it is a non-resource company. An alternative test used by the Exchange is a maximum market capitalization test. This test requires the company to have a market capitalization, excluding any escrow shares, of less than $100,000.00 if it is a resource company or $150,000.00 if it is a non-resource company. It must be stressed that the company must meet all of these requirements or be one which would shortly satisfy each of these criteria in the absence of the proposed reorganization. The reason for this latitude is that the Exchange will not, in essence, force a company to become essentially insolvent before allowing it to be reorganized within the meaning of the subject Listings Policy Statement.

To satisfy the requirement of being reorganized within the meaning of Listings Policy Statement No. 17, the listed company must meet three criteria established by the Exchange. The listed company must effect either a private placement or a public distribution of its securities, either pursuant to an SMF or by way of a rights offering, the proceeds of which must be sufficient to adequately fund the company's recommended work program or business plan, and at least two of the following: the election or appointment of a majority of new principals, the acquisition of a resource property or other asset by the company, a share consolidation or other capital reorganization resulting from a new business combination or the satisfaction of most of the company's debt, by way of share issuance or otherwise. The effect of all of the above must be that the company will meet the following of the Exchange's listing requirements. First, the company must exceed the listing maintenance requirement for shareholder distribution (see Chapter 17). Second, it must have acquired a property of merit satisfactory to the Exchange. This requirement differs from the initial listing requirement prescribing that a listed company must have a property on which certain minimum expenditures have been made. Third, the company must have adequate working capital and funding to carry out its business plan or recommended work program. These, it should be noted, are in marked contrast to the Exchange's initial listing requirements.

B. General Requirements

There are five general requirements associated with issuing additional principals' shares to the principals of resource companies. There is one tolerance permitted in connection with their issuance, and that is that an inactive listed company may issue additional principals' shares even though it may have outstanding principals' or escrow shares and even though it did not have, at the time if first went public, any outstanding principals' or escrow shares. These particular terms form part of the subject Listings Policy Statement because, prior to its initial publication in late 1984, the Superintendent of Brokers' policy was prohibitive on at least one, if not both, of these points. The five general requirements are primarily prohibitive in nature. The first requirement prescribes that additional principals' shares may be sold only for cash and that each principal must pay cash for these additional principals' shares. The second requirement is that additional principals' shares may only be issued and transferred to persons who, or their majority-owned companies which, satisfy the definition of principal, that is, directors, senior officers and promoters of the listed company. The third requirement provides for a written agreement governing the issuance of the shares to be entered into at the time the reorganization occurs but prohibits the actual issuance of the shares until the reorganization has been completed. This requirement is significant because it means the issuance will form an incentive to the principals to complete the reorganization but, at the same time, prohibit them from voting those shares during the reorganization process itself.

The fourth requirement deals with the matter of how many times a listed company may issue additional principals' shares. It is an important restriction because the treatment will, in a very direct way, limit the reorganization of companies which have their shares listed for trading on the Exchange. The Special Committee decided to approach the problem from the number of times that the same principal could receive additional principals' shares of one listed company. The policy prohibits the issuance of additional principals' shares to one time only if the principal has previously owned, or currently owns, principals' or escrow shares of the listed company or twice if he has not previously owned, or currently owns, principals' or escrow shares of the same company. In bottom line terms, this means that the same principal may only receive principals' shares of the same company two times. It should be noted here that the words principals' shares as used in this Chapter do not refer to all principals' shares of listed companies. Rather, they refer to principals' shares which are issued pursuant to Securities Commission Local Policy Statement No. 3-07 (February 6, 1987) or the 750,000 escrow shares which were issued in consideration of a resource property interest pursuant to a predecessor Local Policy Statement to Local Policy Statement No. 3-07. The term also excludes earn-out shares issued under the same Local Policy Statement No. 3-07.

The fifth and final requirement is that the principals acquiring the additional principals' shares must execute and file with the Exchange an agreement governing the escrow provisions applying to the principals' shares which must be in the form attached as Schedule "A" to Securities Commission Local Policy Statement No. 3-07 (February 6, 1987) with one exception. The agreement must provide for cancellation of any principals' shares not released from escrow after five years from the date the Exchange accepts the agreement for filing.

C. Maximum Number of Shares

The maximum number of additional principals' shares which may be issued by a listed company being reorganized depends on whether there are any existing principals' or escrow shares outstanding and whether a share consolidation is involved in the reorganization, and, if so, on the ratio of the consolidation. The total number of additional principals' shares which may be issued is limited to the difference between the total number of existing principals' or escrow shares outstanding and the following:

Consolidation Ratio	Number
none	750,000
1:2	656,250
1:3	562,500
1:4	468,750
1:5 (and greater)	375,000

For example, if the listed company currently has 412,500 principals' shares outstanding (the number of remaining escrow shares a typical listed company would have after three 15% releases), and had a capital alteration as part of its reorganization in the form of a "one new for three old" share consolidation, then it would be limited to issuing 150,000 additional principals' shares, that number being the difference between the allowable number of additional principals' shares in the case of a 1:3 share consolidation, namely 562,500, and the existing number of principals' shares, namely 412,500. This particular company may also have 1,000,000 earn-out shares outstanding after the share consolidation if 3,000,000 such shares were issued and outstanding before the consolidation making for a total of 1,562,000 escrow shares after the reorganization had been completed.

D. Minimum Issuance Price

There are several restrictions contained in Listings Policy Statement No. 17 dealing with the minimum issuance price of additional principals' shares. The key factor relates to the market price of the company's shares prior to the date of the agreement providing for the issuance of the additional principals' shares. A subordinate factor is whether a share consolidation is involved in the reorganization.

The over-riding minimum issuance price which must be used is the greater of $0.01 and 10% of the market price of the company's shares. The market price of the company's shares is deemed by the Exchange to be the average closing price of the company's shares, as traded on the Exchange, during the 20 day period immediately preceding the date of the agreement providing for the issuance of the additional principals' shares. If the reorganization involves a share consolidation, then the minimum issuance price must be calculated by taking the average closing price over the same 20 day period and multiplying it by that number equal to the number of pre-consolidated shares which are required to be exchanged for one consolidated share. For example, if the average trading price is $0.17 and a 1:5 share consolidation is involved in the reorganization, then the minimum issuance price per share is 10% of $0.85.

E. Other Requirements

There are three other special requirements contained in Listings Policy Statement No. 17. First, as referred to above, the term of the additional principals' shares escrow agreement is limited to five years from the date the Exchange accepts the escrow agreement for filing. This is to be compared with the ten year term allowed in the case of initial principals' shares. Second, the issuance of additional principals' shares by an inactive company must be approved by the company's shareholders by a special resolution, which is a majority of not less than 75% of the votes cast by the company's shareholders who vote on the matter. As noted above, the principals who are to receive the additional principals' shares will not be able to vote these shares at that shareholders meeting since the Policy Statement only permits their issuance after the reorganization has been fully completed. Third, the escrow agreement must provide for all rights of cancellation which are provided for in Securities Commission Policy Statement No. 3-07 (February 6, 1987) (see Chapter 2). It should also be noted that the Exchange regards the proposed and actual issuance of additional principals' shares, as well as a reorganization of a listed company, to constitute material changes. Hence, it requires the listed company to issue a news release when these events occur.

ESCROW SHARE RELEASES

In addition to setting forth for the first time the Exchange's written policy dealing with the issuance of additional principals' shares, the Special Committee examined the manner in which the Exchange Listing Committee was exercising its discretion in making orders for the release of escrow and principals' shares. This examination subsequently lead to the publication of Listings Policy Statement No. 18. This area deals with an important subject since the release of escrow or principals' shares will affect the future incentive available to principals and their present financial well being, both of which will have a bearing on the further development of the listed company's assets and eventual profitability. The criteria for the release of principals' shares are set forth in this Listings Policy Statement.

The first rule is that the Exchange will not permit more than two separate pro-rata escrow share releases during any given twelve month period. The second rule is that the Exchange will consent to a release of 15% of the original number of escrow or principals' shares deposited in escrow for every $100,000.00 expended directly on the undertaking of the company. Any expenditures not included in an application may be carried over to a subsequent application. In the case of a resource company, only exploration and development expenditures are relevant; in the case of a non-resource company, only research and development expenditures, and other expenditures specifically related to the corporate undertaking, are relevant. The expenditures which are looked at by the Exchange are only those which are incurred by the listed company after the date a receipt is issued for its prospectus qualifying its initial public offering or after subsequent principals' shares are issued.

The third and fourth rules are, respectively, that the Exchange will only consent to a maximum of 50% of the original number of escrow or principals' shares deposited in escrow during any given twelve month period and is empowered to refuse to order a favourable escrow release, or to otherwise reduce the number of shares to be released, if the listed company's administrative expenses exceed 50% of the expenditures made on the listed company's undertaking. For example, if exploration expenses for a six month period aggregate $300,000.00, and administrative expenses for the same six month period total $200,000.00, the Exchange typically will approve only a 30% pro-rata escrow release. If, in our example, exploration expenses were $200,000.00, only a 15% pro-rata escrow release would be approved.

The fifth rule, implicit in Listings Policy Statement No. 18, is that all escrow releases are made on a pro-rata basis. This is the case unless all affected parties, including the listed company, agree to the contrary.

If an applicant company's securities are or remain in the course of a distribution, as would be the case if it has trading warrants or agents' warrants outstanding, then the Exchange will seek the consent of the company's agents or underwriters, as the case may be. This is done not to protect the broker's interests but to ensure that the release and subsequent resale into the open market by the escrow shareholders will not operate to the economic detriment of the listed company.

When determining the applicable expenditures to be considered, the Exchange generally will consider only the financial statements, including Quarterly Reports, which have been filed with the Exchange. Where necessary, a listed company may supply additional financial information to support its application or may be ordered by the Exchange to do so. The company, or its filing solicitor, must identify in the release application letter what source of financial information is being relied upon by the applicant company.

For the most part, persons holding escrow or principals' shares will form part of the management of the listed company. This however can change over time and therefore it is not unusual that some of the escrow or principals' shares come to be held by members outside the management group. In these situations, the loyalty to the company of the non-management shareholder may disappear and the Exchange may have to deal with a contested release application. By contested is meant a situation where the management of the listed company opposes an application brought on by non-management holders of escrow or principals' shares. In these circumstances, the Exchange will seek the written representations of both sides of the argument and will then consider five, often opposing, elements and render a decision based on the written representations.

The first element for consideration is the nature of the escrow under review, including an assessment of any transfers within escrow and the basis of any Exchange consent given to such transfers. Second, the Exchange will consider the interests of the applicant for release and third will consider the interests of the listed company in opposing the release. Fourth, the Exchange must consider the interests of the then current shareholders where the interests may differ from those of the listed company and its management and, finally, must consider the interests of the investing public generally or, in different words, future investors in the company. These often bitterly fought applications are few and far between, however, when they do occur, it is not unusual to find the Exchange's decision appealed. Two such cases are *In the Matter of Cusac Industries Ltd.*, Corporate and Financial Services Commission (November 25, 1983) and *In the Matter of Beaver Resources Inc.*, Corporate and Financial Services Commission (October 9, 1985). In both cases, the listed company's opposition to the escrow release was based on its position that it was arranging a financing, and that a release and subsequent resale of the escrow shares would impair the company's ability to complete the financing or, at a minimum, would result in greater dilution to all of the company's shareholders than if the financing were completed before the release. In both cases, the Exchange's decision was upheld by the Corporate and Financial Services Commission.

CHAPTER FIFTEEN

Loan and Loan Guarantee Bonuses, Finder's Fees and Commissions

LOAN AND LOAN GUARANTEE BONUSES

A listed company borrowing funds or, obtaining a guarantee for a loan may be required to offer an incentive to procure the loan or guarantee. A Resource or Commercial/Industrial Company is free to negotiate the amount of this incentive. However, in an effort to assist management in determining what might be acceptable, the Exchange, by Listings Policy Statement No. 6, has established guidelines for the granting of bonuses to lenders or guarantors of a listed company through the issuance of shares or share purchase warrants. The guideline must be strictly adhered to by Venture Companies. The policy was originally introduced on February 3, 1983 and has undergone several modifications to its present form. It is the inherent responsibility of management to negotiate the best possible agreement for the listed company using the parameters of Listings Policy Statement No. 6 as a guideline.

The granting of a bonus for a loan or guarantee is permitted in arm's length and non-arm's length transactions and, in the case of the latter, the Exchange is particularly concerned that management acts in good faith in negotiating the bonus with the interest of the company taking precedence over self-interest. In approving the bonus, the Exchange will require confirmation of three matters. First, the listed company must demonstrate the need for the loan and that the loan or guarantee, as the case may be, would not have been granted had a bonus not been given to the lender or guarantor. Second, the interest charged on such a loan should be set at a rate no higher than the rate applicable to bank consumer loans under similar circumstances. Third, the Exchange must be assured that the lender or guarantor receives only one bonus from the company for a specific loan transaction. This is referred to as the once-in-a-lifetime rule.

The listed company must give the Exchange prompt notice of the loan transaction and, where the transaction represents a change that would reasonably be expected to affect the market value of the company's securities, timely disclosure of the material particulars of the transaction to the public by way of a news release must also be made.

Shares issued as a bonus may be freely tradeable as far as the Exchange is concerned, regardless of whether the transaction is at arm's length. Similarly, shares issued on exercise of the share purchase warrant, which itself must be non-transferable, will be freely tradeable. The shares issued as a bonus, pursuant to the exercise of the share purchase warrant or otherwise, must be, at a minimum, valued using the average market price of the company's shares over a two week period preceding the date the funds are loan or guaranteed.

The value of the shares issued as a bonus must not exceed 5% of the amount of funds loaned or guaranteed, based upon the average market price. Where a listed company negotiates a bonus in the form of a share purchase warrant, the shares which may be acquired on exercise of the warrant must not exceed, in value, 10% of the amount loaned or guaranteed and may be exercisable for the earlier of two years or the term of the loan. The warrant must provide, however, that if the loan is reduced or paid out prior to the expiry of the warrant, and if one year of the warrant term has elapsed, the warrant must terminate 30 days after the satisfaction of the loan or must be proportionately reduced 30 days after the loan has been reduced. The exercise price must be at least equal to the average market price of the company shares over the two week period referred to above, and must be escalated by a 15% premium if the warrant has an exercise term exceeding one year.

The Exchange recognizes that the payment of a larger bonus may be justified where, for instance, the company's ability to repay a loan is not evident or where a guarantee represents the sole collateral for a loan. In these situations, a bonus of freely tradeable shares may have a value of up to 20% of the amount loan or guaranteed, based on the average market price. The non-transferable share purchase warrant may entitle the holder to shares valued at 40% of the amount loaned or guaranteed. The other terms of this warrant are the same as are discussed above.

FINDER'S FEES AND COMMISSIONS

The Exchange has further regulated by policy, in Listings Policy Statement No. 6, the payment of finder's fees or commissions to those involved in transactions which, through their efforts, result in a measurable benefit to the listed company. The benefit, however, must be received by the company (such as proceeds from a private placement and the acquisition or sale of an asset) and, accordingly, the finder's fee or commission cannot be paid until the transaction has been completed. The Exchange will not favourably consider a proposal to pay a finder's fee or commission for services or benefits which have not yet been received by the listed company.

Unlike the payment of a bonus for a loan or guarantee, a finder's fee or commission may not be paid where the finder or agent is not at arm's length (is an insider) with the company and its management. This prohibition does not include a payment to a finder or agent who may have been specifically retained by the company to locate, acquire or facilitate a transaction which results in a benefit to the company which the company would not have obtained without the finder or agent.

The Exchange's policy restates the Rules of the Exchange which strictly prohibit the payment of any direct or indirect compensation to a registered representative, trader, assistant trader (as defined in the Rules of the Exchange) or employee of a Member for acting as a finder or an agent of a listed company in the acquisition or sale of properties or other assets, unless the prior approval of the Exchange's Board of Governors has been obtained (see Chapter 12). This prohibition does not apply to the payment of such compensation to Members or to directors, officers or partners of Members. The revisions made to the subject Exchange Rules in September, 1985 included the extension of this prohibition to those individuals who are employed by, or perform the same functions as a registered representative, trader or assistant trader at, brokerage firms which are not Members of the Exchange. The net effect of this prohibition is that it extends to such individuals no matter where they are resident. The Exchange is of the view that it is in the public interest to apply this policy to such individuals whether or not they are employed by Members of the Exchange. As discussed in Chapters 4 and 12, the Corporate and Financial Services Commission *In The Matter of Mariah Resources Ltd.* (December 21, 1984), did not interfere with the Exchange's decision to refuse the conditional listing application of Mariah Resources Ltd. on grounds which included the involvement of a stock broker in the United States selling a resource property interest to Mariah Resources Ltd. in consideration of shares and cash.

A finder's fee or commission may be paid in the form of cash, shares, share purchase warrants or an interest in the acquired assets. The Exchange developed certain guidelines and criteria for the payment of finder's fees and commissions as set forth in Listings Policy Statement No. 6 which must be adhered to by Venture Companies. The finder's fee or commission, if stated in dollars, should be a percentage of the value of the benefit received by the listed company within the following parameters:

Benefit Received	Value of Finder's Fee/Commission
on the first $300,000.00	up to 10%
$300,000.00 to $1,000,000.00	up to 7.5%
$1,000,000.00 and over	up to 5%

The Exchange suggests that the percentages be scaled down as the value of the benefit increases over $1,000,000.00.

In November, 1988, the Exchange deregulated the underwriting discounts and agency fees which its Members could receive when involved with listed companies effecting Exchange offerings made through the facilities of the Exchange. In early January, 1989, the Exchange announced that this same deregulatory posture had been applied to the policies relating to bonuses, finder's fees and commissions payable to Members of the Exchange. Accordingly, while the general provisions of Listings Policy Statement No. 6 apply to Members, it does not in any way regulate the amount of compensation payable.

It is worth considering an example of a calculation of a finder's fee. If a person arranges a private placement for $1,500,000.00, the finder's fee payable may be as high as $107,500.00, being 10% of the first $300,000.00 ($30,000.00), 7.5% of the next $700,000.00 ($52,500.00) and 5% of the remaining $500,000.00 ($25,000.00). Accordingly, although the benefit is over $1,000,000.00, the finder's fee is not required to be limited to 5% of the aggregate amount.

With respect to the acquisition or disposition of resource properties or other assets which may not have a determinate value, the value of the property or asset for purposes of a finder's fee or commission is generally the value of the acquisition costs or disposition proceeds. In the case of the acquisition of a natural resource property by an option agreement which may involve staged option payments and share issuances from the listed company, as well as a series of expenditure commitments, the value of the property may be determined to be the aggregate of all option payments and share consideration to the optionor plus the expenditure commitments. The fee or commission, however, may only be paid when the option payments are made, the shares are issued and the expenditure commitments are satisfied. The Exchange appears to prefer that the finder's fee be based on the considerable payable and expenditures required in the first year of the option term only.

Where shares of the listed company are to be issued as a finder's fee or a commission, the shares are to be valued at the average market price of the company's shares for the two weeks preceding the event which gave rise to the fee or commission. However, the value must not be less than $0.15 per share. In the case of a private placement, the value of the shares generally will be the undiscounted value of the company's shares on which the private placement price was based. Where the consideration is being paid for negotiating a transaction, the share value is generally based on the two week average market price prior to concluding negotiations. Where the services are in the form of locating or arranging an acquisition, the value of the shares issued for the finder's fee or commission is generally based on the two week average prior to an agreement in principle being reached and is not based on the two week period which precedes a formal agreement being executed or regulatory approval being obtained to the transaction.

If a listed company chooses to issue a non-transferable share purchase warrant as the finder's fee or commission, the shares to be acquired on exercise are valued on the basis of the two week average market price as determined above. However, the benefit in terms of the call amount on the shares to the finder or agent may be up to double that which could be paid in the form of cash, shares or an interest in the asset. In other words, the recipient of a warrant would be entitled to acquire twice as many shares under a warrant as the recipient would receive if shares were issued as the fee or commission. The term of such warrant must not exceed two years. The exercise price of the warrant in the first year must be at least equal to the two week average market price and must be escalated by a 15% premium over that price in the second year.

CHAPTER SIXTEEN

Acquisitions and Amalgamations

GENERAL

Perhaps because the topic is broad and complex, the Exchange has never published any rules or regulations dealing with the subject of acquisitions, the acquiring of an asset by a listed company. There are those who argue that a written policy is needed to ensure uniformity and equality of the application of the Exchange's discretion in dealing with a variety of property or asset acquisitions. There are those who argue to the contrary, asserting that the Exchange's discretion would become too rigid and inflexible thence detrimental to the venture capital market. Whatever the reason, the fact remains that the Exchange does not have a written policy dealing with acquisitions. It does, however, have an unwritten policy, which is evident by the number and variety of documents disclosing acquisitions the Exchange routinely accepts, or rejects, for filing. The unwritten policy is based on practice, and it is that practice which is dealt with in this Chapter. It should be remembered that the Exchange has a written prohibition against brokers generally selling assets to, or buying assets from, listed companies; it also has prescribed certain requirements where a vendor of property or assets is a director, senior officer or promoter, or any of their associates, of the listed company acquiring the property or assets (see Chapter 12).

There are a number of basic principles which the Exchange utilizes in vetting acquisitions. The Exchange values any non-escrow shares being issued as having a value equal to their number multiplied by the per share market price of the company's shares as traded on the Exchange on the day the agreement was entered into. In making this calculation the Exchange does not take into account the capitalization or public float of a particular listed company. This is sometimes considered anomalous since different percentages of the outstanding voting shares of a listed company may be exchanged for the same assets. With small value asset purchases this is not a problem but where the asset has a significant value, the apparent anomaly becomes noticeable. Regardless, the Exchange uses the market price, without discount, to ascertain the value of any non-escrowed shares being issued by a listed company.

The value of the consideration which the listed company proposes to pay for an asset should be, more or less, equal to or less than, the value of the asset. Here, the Exchange is applying more of a fair, just and equitable doctrine as opposed to the unconscionability doctrine referred to in paragraph 120(2)(b) of the *Regulation to the Securities Act*. That is, the Exchange analyzes an asset transaction in terms of the basic fairness of the transaction as opposed to rejecting a filing only where it thinks an unconscionable consideration is proposed to be paid by the listed company.

A vendor must be expected to share the same level of risk which the vendor is asking the listed company to assume. This is the premise behind the Exchange's "four by fifty" option rule, to be discussed presently, which it utilizes in the case of the acquisition by listed companies of undeveloped mineral properties. This principle leads to the proposition that the listed company will not be permitted to give up something of value for something with no apparent value. It also means that the value of both, that is the value of the thing being acquired and the value of the consideration being paid, must be at least the same. For example if an individual, on an arm's length basis, proposes to sell some mining claims which were recently staked at a cost of $5,000.00 to a listed company for non-escrowed shares having an aggregate market value far in excess of the staking cost, then the Exchange would not accept that transaction unless it could be firmly established that the mining claims constitute a property of merit. Similarly, if unproven intellectual property is proposed to be sold to a listed company in return for free-trading shares far in excess of the development costs to date of the intellectual property, the Exchange will refuse to accept the transaction. The same principle has lead the Exchange to develop, in conjunction with the Superintendent of Brokers, the concept of earn-out shares. The two securities regulators are trying to prevent a vendor from being in a position to realize a profit on a particular transaction which otherwise has no demonstrable benefit to the listed company until, in fact, the listed company has received a pre-determined, quantifiable benefit from the transaction.

The Exchange has developed a general reluctance to approve what are called flip transactions, even in arm's length situations. The disclosure provisions of the Exchange's Filing Statement form and the SMF form, Form 24 under the *Securities Act*, require disclosure of the cost of a natural resource property, or a non-resource asset, to a vendor if he has acquired it in the year prior to dealing it to a listed company. While the Exchange will permit what it considers to be a reasonable profit on such a transaction, it will not allow a larger one, unless there are unusual circumstances, based on the argument of the listed company that the vendor obtained the property at a bargain price or at below market cost.

The Exchange applies the same shareholder approval rule which applies in the case of private placements to property or other asset acquisitions. In other words if one person, or group acting together, is to receive more than 20% of the outstanding voting shares of the listed company, such 20% being calculated on a post-transaction basis, then the listed company's shareholders will be required by the Exchange to approve the whole transaction.

The Exchange operates on the basis that the onus of establishing the benefit and value of the asset to the listed company lies with the listed company. This is significant because it means that the listed company must prove, as it were, its case to the satisfaction of the Exchange. Moreover it means that the Exchange is of the view that it does not have to disprove the case presented. This situation is different from most regulatory forums where the onus of establishing a prejudicial case usually lies with the regulator, not the entity being regulated. The application of this principle can prove difficult in some cases and even can prevent a listed company from proceeding further in other cases. As an example, a vendor is not usually legally obligated to supply details requested by the Exchange to a listed company for transmittal to the Exchange. Certainly the Exchange has no authoritative jurisdiction to compel such disclosure. If the vendor refuses and insists on maintaining his legal right to privacy, the Exchange may not accept the filing.

Finally, the fact that a transaction has been made in a negotiated arm's length atmosphere, or that the listed company's shareholders have approved the transaction by special resolution or otherwise, does not carry any significant weight with the Exchange. Whether or not this should be the case is debatable; nevertheless, it must be recognized.

MINERAL PROPERTIES

A. General

For the most part, the types of mineral properties acquired by companies listed on the Exchange are divided into three categories. These are undeveloped mineral properties; properties of merit; and proven-up properties. A proven-up property is a resource property which has drill-indicated ore reserves, or proven reserves of recoverable oil or gas, and is fairly easy to value. They form the basis of only a few transactions and consequently will not be discussed here. The other two categories of natural resource properties, while harder to value, routinely form the basis of listed company requests. It is these two categories on which the following discussion will focus.

B. Undeveloped Mineral Property

The Exchange, over time, has developed the four by fifty option rule. This unwritten rule provides that where a 100% interest in an undeveloped mineral property is to be acquired by a listed company, the total share consideration which may be given in exchange for the property will be limited to four blocks of 50,000 shares each. In most cases, the Exchange will permit the up-front issuance of 50,000 shares once it has approved the transaction. The one situation where the Exchange will object to the initial issuance of 50,000 shares is where the market value of those shares, so-called free-trading shares, is significantly out of line with the total cost of the first phase of exploration work. In this case the Exchange will require a reduction in the number of up-front shares to what it considers to be a more reasonable amount. The Exchange will, however, permit the up-front payment of cash to allow the vendor to recoup out-of-pocket costs such as staking costs, acquisition costs and any exploration costs incurred to date. The subsequent issuance of 50,000 share blocks must be tied to the completion and recommendation of further phases of exploration or development work on the property. For example, a typical arrangement would see 50,000 shares issued at the end of the first phase of exploration so long as the undertaking of the second phase was recommended, etc. Before the issuance of additional blocks of 50,000 shares, the Exchange requires that engineering reports, prepared by qualified independent engineers, be filed with and accepted by the Exchange. As part of these transactions the Exchange usually permits the listed company to assume any financial obligations required either to keep the property in good standing or to otherwise maintain rights to the property. The Exchange will also permit the reservation of certain royalties to the vendor of the property. In the case of a net smelter return, the Exchange usually will allow only a 5% return. In the case of a net profits interest, a maximum royalty of between 15% and 20% may be permitted.

Where the interest being acquired is less than a 100% interest, the Exchange generally scales down the amount of consideration, in terms of shares or otherwise, in proportion to the interest being acquired. Similarly, the Exchange will try to prevent a vendor from breaking up a property, the sole purpose of which is to enter into as many four by fifty option agreements as the vendor can, thus securing more shares than should ordinarily be the case.

C. Resource Property of Merit

A resource property will be classified by the Exchange as being a property of merit, sometimes called a property of unusual merit, if recent extensive exploration work has been carried out with favourable results or in other cases where recent preliminary extensive exploration work shows the same geological characteristics present on the property as are present on an adjacent property where the adjacent property has proven or near-proven tonnages of ore associated with it. This situation is to be distinguished from the property which is merely a good location bet. The so-called theory of closeology does not render a natural resource property a property of merit simply because it is close, or even adjacent, to properties which have drill-indicated reserves of ore.

If the property is regarded by the Exchange as a property of merit, then it will permit additional share consideration (i.e. in addition to that which may be paid for an undeveloped property) to be issued by the listed company but, except in rare cases, only where this additional issuance takes place concurrently with or after the commencement of commercial production. This additional consideration is usually limited to the issuance of an additional 100,000 shares on the commencement of commercial production. The Exchange is stringent on not normally permitting an increase in the previously described maximum levels of net smelter return and net profits interest.

NON-RESOURCE PROPERTIES OR ASSETS

A. General

The Exchange has, in the last few years, accepted and adopted the broad set of non-resource property acquisition principles, and some related rules, which the Securities Commission expresses in its Local Policy Statement No. 3-07 (February 6, 1987). This particular Local Policy Statement divides assets into two, quite distinct categories: determinate value assets and indeterminate value assets. In each category there are further delineations. The Exchange maintains this particular classification scheme to analyze non-resource acquisitions.

A determinate value asset is said to have a hard or soft value, although these words do not appear in the Securities Commission's Policy Statement, and indeterminate value assets may be assets of unusual merit. By far the largest category of asset acquisitions by companies which have their securities listed on the Exchange is of soft value, determinate value assets. Before proceeding to define what these terms mean and the rules associated with them, it is wise to consider what the Exchange does not regard as a property or asset for the purpose of its acquisition rules. The list of non-properties comprises ideas, principles, practices or devices which are not patentable or otherwise distinguishable from common skill or knowledge. This precludes what were in the past commonly called concept companies from being listed on the Exchange, although it does not otherwise operate to prevent companies being listed which are at a very early stage in their asset development.

B. Determinate Value Assets

As noted above, there are two, quite distinct types of asset category subsumed in this type of asset. A determinate value asset is said to have a hard value where its fair market value can be determined by the application of generally recognized valuation techniques. Real estate is a good example of this type of asset. The acquisition rule of the Exchange is fairly straightforward in these circumstances. As long as the consideration proposed to be paid by the listed company does not exceed the fair market value of the asset, the Exchange will approve the transaction. Where shares of the listed company are to be issued, these shares may be free of any earn-out restrictions. The maximum number of shares which may be issued by the listed company will depend upon the actual market price of the listed company's shares as traded on the day the listed company entered into the transaction. The Exchange does not permit the use of discounts in making these calculations. This is anomalous when one considers that an acquisition transaction is, except for the nature of the consideration being paid to the listed company, identical in substance to that of a private placement.

A determinate value asset is said to have a soft value when its fair market value cannot be determined objectively, but can be estimated by the use of some assessment or estimate of future earnings potential. Almost without exception, if the value of an asset is being determined by a capitalization of earnings derived from projected sales and expense figures, then, so long as the assumptions are reasonable and are supported by sufficient direct and specific evidence, the asset will be said to have a soft value. In these situations, the Exchange requires that any shares to be issued not be issued until they are earned, or, if they are to be issued, then they must be held in escrow and only released from the escrow as they are earned.

Where shares are escrowed on an earn-out basis, they are released on a cash flow basis, using as the determinant for release the market price of the listed company's shares on the day the agreement was entered into by the listed company. For example, if the market price on the day the agreement was reached by the parties was $0.50 per share, then the Exchange will permit the release of one of the listed company's shares from escrow for every $0.50 cash flow realized by the listed company as a result of acquiring the asset. It should be noted that by cash flow, the Exchange means net profits, after tax, as calculated in accordance with generally accepted accounting principles and adjusted for any non-cash items such as depletion, depreciation, amortization of goodwill, amortization of research and development costs and deferred taxes. The Exchange permits the earn-out period to be up to a maximum of six years.

The numerical limit on the maximum total number of earn-out shares which the Exchange will permit to be issued depends upon the circumstances of each case and the value of the asset being acquired by the listed company. However, the actual number of earn-out shares must be the subject of an opinion by an independent, qualified expert to the effect that the total number of shares is not unconscionable and is otherwise defensible.

In most transactions, there are elements of each type of asset. For example, where a listed company acquires all the outstanding shares of a private company so that it becomes a wholly owned subsidiary of the listed company, the private company may have some hard value assets. In these situations, the Exchange will permit a combination of earn-out and non-escrowed shares to be issued. Alternatively, and if the listed company has sufficient cash reserves, the hard asset value portion of the transaction may be paid for in cash rather than by the issuance of non-escrowed shares by the listed company.

C. Indeterminate Value Assets

Assets which have not been sufficiently developed to permit any meaningful analysis of market potential are categorized by the Exchange as having indeterminate value. These types of asset acquisitions are quite rare since most listed companies acquire one form or another of determinate value assets. Where the asset has this character, no up-front consideration may be paid by a listed company unless the vendor can establish out-of-pocket costs. The Exchange will generally restrict the acquisition in the same manner that it regulates the acquisition of undeveloped resource properties. That is, a 200,000 share limit will be imposed prior to the asset having demonstrated its commercial viability.

AMALGAMATIONS

It may seem odd to some that a discussion of amalgamations would be covered in the same chapter as acquisitions. However, the fact is the Exchange views amalgamations which involve a listed company amalgamating with either another listed company or a private company as a type of acquisition by the listed company.

The Exchange has a rather strict, although straight-forward unwritten policy. It determines the relative values of both companies and then, after having made that determination, assesses what relative number of shares of the amalgamated company each shareholder group should obtain. For example, if A Company and B Company are amalgamating to form C Company, and if the value ascribed by the Exchange to A Company represents 60% of the value of C Company, which latter value is calculated by adding the value of A Company and B Company, than A Company's shareholders should get 60% of the initial outstanding capital of C Company. The significance of the application of this unwritten policy is that the Exchange values a listed company based on its issued capitalization multiplied by its market price per share. The Exchange does not look at its assets or consider the nature of its assets. The Exchange's argument is based on the notion that a chancered price in an open market is the determinative value, irrespective of book value. In the case of non-listed or private companies, the Exchange usually looks at its book value, although in some cases the Exchange has ascribed a total value to it based on the price per share of recent share sales for cash consideration. Alternatively, if a valuation of the private company has been prepared, and there is a hard determinate value, or other fair market value, then these latter values may be used. These situations are few and far between. If the private company has escrow shares (principal's or escrow earn-out shares) or earn-out shares outstanding, then the Exchange may require these shares to be cancelled as part of the transaction, otherwise, the escrow shareholders will be required to receive escrow shares in return. On occasion the Exchange will permit the issuance by the amalgamated company of earn-out shares to the shareholders of the private company if it owns assets of a determinate value, soft value nature which were acquired by the private company from those shareholders. The application of the book value method for valuing private companies can often result in the Exchange refusing to approve an amalgamation between a listed company, which may be a shell company, and a private company having assets of not insignificant worth or potential, even in instances when the shareholders of both companies have approved the amalgamation terms and the British Columbia Supreme Court has approved the terms of the amalgamation agreement (as required by the *Company Act*). Using the principle of comparative values, the Exchange has little difficulty in assessing the merit of amalgamations between two listed companies.

CHAPTER SEVENTEEN

Reactivations

GENERAL

In late 1988, the Special Policy Committee was struck to see what, among other things, should be done about the rapidly increasing number of inactive, listed companies. The concern was that while new listings continued to occur at a relatively high rate given the state of the local venture capital equity market, many listed companies, after having expended the funds raised in their initial public offering, were unable to raise further funds. As a consequence of this inability to raise funds, the companies involved, unless taken over by new principals, would quickly become insolvent and trading in their securities would be suspended by the Exchange. These securities would, in the absence of a reorganization or reactivation of their business affairs, eventually be delisted from trading on the Exchange.

The Special Policy Committee focused on what it felt were the two main reasons why inactive companies were not being reactivated under the then-existing securities regulatory scheme. It determined that the Exchange had developed a practice of requiring all the stages involved in reactivations to be done as essentially one transaction. It was determined also that the Exchange's initial listing standards had become outdated in the sense that the key minimum thresholds had become, over time, relatively low. The combination of these two factors had the practical effect of driving new business opportunities into new companies which would then finance the undertaking by conducting an initial public offering. The Special Policy Committee recommended that the Exchange's initial listing requirements be changed to those discussed in Chapter 3. As a corollary, that Committee also recommended changes which lead to a revised Listings Policy Statement No. 17, a significant portion of which was discussed in Chapter 14. The Special Policy Committee's recommendation also lead to the establishment of minimum listing maintenance standards, which will form the topic for discussion in the latter part of this Chapter. The significant policy change which resulted from the Committee's work was the relaxation of certain of the Exchange's policies to inactive listed companies and the creation of a special type of private placement. These, and related matters, will form the subject of the present discussion.

TRADING COMPANIES

A. General

Exchange Listings Policy Statement No. 17 distinguishes between trading companies, that is, listed companies which have their securities listed, posted and called for trading on the Exchange and those which do not, which are called non-trading companies and are dealt with below.

A trading company which falls within the definition of an inactive company in the Policy Statement (see Chapter 14) either may be declared an inactive company by the Exchange or voluntarily elect to be treated by the Exchange as an inactive company. A company may be deemed inactive, or may elect to be treated as if it were inactive, based solely on the market capitalization test set forth in the Policy Statement.

Once declared to be inactive, the listed company must comply fully with the Exchange's minimum listing maintenance requirements within one year of the time it achieves its inactive status. It must subsequently meet standards very close to initial listing standards, although there is no time requirement within which the company must meet these standards. It initiates the process by filing with the Exchange, within 90 days of being declared inactive, either an acceptable submission demonstrating that it is proceeding with the reorganization or an acceptable plan outlining the steps it proposes to take to achieve maintenance standing. A failure to make such a submission will result in the company's listed securities being suspended from trading on the Exchange. A failure by the company to attain the Exchange's minimum listing maintenance requirements in the one year period will also result in the Exchange suspending trading in the company's listed securities.

Once the company has attained the levels prescribed by the Exchange's minimum listing maintenance requirements, it is expected to carry out the balance of its reorganization. The Exchange has set no time period within which a company must complete its reorganization. However, if the company fails to maintain the prescribed minimum levels for listing maintenance purposes and is once again deemed to be inactive, the Exchange will suspend trading in its listed securities, with the result that the company will become a non-trading company.

There is a special restriction which attaches to all trading, inactive companies. This restriction applies from the time the company has been declared inactive to the time it fully completes its reorganization. The restriction is that the company may not grant new incentive stock options and its existing principals are prohibited from exercising previously granted incentive stock options. The Exchange may, in its discretion, permit new incentive stock options to be granted and previously granted unexpired options to be exercised by principals providing the reorganization has been substantially completed. This prohibition applies after the company has ceased to be inactive (by virtue of its having attained minimum listing maintenance status) and up to the point when its reorganization has either been completed or, with the Exchange's consent, substantially completed.

B. Effect of Reorganization

An inactive company must undergo a reorganization, as detailed in Chapter 14, the effect of which must be to bring the company into compliance with certain Exchange requirements. As expressed in Listings Policy Statement No. 17, the company must meet three essential requirements, after it has initially met the Exchange's minimum listing maintenance requirements. First, the company need only meet the minimum listing maintenance requirement, not the initial listing requirement, for shareholder distribution. Second, the company must, as part of the reorganization, either acquire or maintain a property or asset of merit satisfactory to the Exchange, not a property or asset meeting the initial listing requirements (minimum prior expenditures on the property or asset, etc.). Third, the company must have adequate working capital and funding to carry out its business plan or recommended work program, not the prescribed amount of unallocated working capital required by the Exchange's initial listing requirements.

C. Special Policy Relief

As noted in the beginning of this Chapter, the Special Policy Committee found that one of the major impediments facing listed companies undertaking reactivations in the past was the Exchange's requirement of having all the stages involved in the reorganization to be done as part of one large transaction. Practically speaking, the management of listed companies were not able to comply with this partly written, partly unwritten rule since the various parties to the transaction were unable, in most cases, to cooperate for the period of time required to negotiate and enter the various transactions and then await Exchange acceptance of the various transactions.

Five special policy changes, applicable only to inactive companies, were enacted to deal with this situation: the Exchange's share consolidation (see

Chapter 10) was relaxed so as not to require inactive companies to satisfy all of the Exchange's minimum maintenance listing requirements immediately after the share consolidation. Instead, the inactive company need only meet the Exchange's minimum listing maintenance distribution requirements immediately after the share consolidation. In the case of arm's length shares for debt issuances, while all the provisions of Listings Policy Statement No. 8 apply (see Chapter 11), the company need not demonstrate that it will have a positive working capital position after the share issuance or that the share issuance will necessarily enable the company to secure additional financing or continue as a going concern. In addition, the Exchange may, in its discretion, waive the 1,000,000 share limit imposed in Listings Policy Statement No. 8. While all requirements of Listings Policy Statement No. 11 dealing with the private placement of equity shares apply, the minimum issuance price when a share consolidation is concurrently involved is to be determined by multiplying $0.05, rather than $0.07, by the consolidation ratio. The $0.15 minimum price level continues to apply in this situation. Working capital financings, conducted either as an Exchange offering under an SMF or a rights offering, are permitted where the funds derived from these offerings will be used to finance the costs of the reorganization and will provide sufficient funds to achieve maintenance standing.

The final special policy change saw the creation of what is called a reactivation financing. This financing, a one-time private placement, is restricted to 400,000 shares in total, and these shares may only be purchased by directors and officers of the inactive company. The minimum price per share must be the greater of market price or $0.15. No discounts from the market price may be used to calculate the minimum price per share, nor are options permitted. No hold period is imposed, however, 75% of the total number of shares must be pooled. These pooled shares may be released in three equal share blocks every 90 days after the private placement has been entered into. This special one-time reactivation financing may only be used by an inactive company from the earlier of 120 days from the company being deemed inactive or upon completion of the reorganization. All of the requirements of Listings Policy Statement No. 11 (see Chapter 8) apply to this private placement except those which may conflict with those matters discussed above.

NON-TRADING COMPANIES

Non-trading companies, that is, dormant but listed companies which have their listed securities suspended from trading by the Exchange will, more often than not, be deemed to be dormant as that term is defined in

Securities Commission Local Policy Statement No. 3-35 (October 13, 1989). In order for a company to comply with this Local Policy Statement, the company must bring itself into good standing with the Registrar of Companies, and into good reporting standing with both the Exchange and the Superintendent of Brokers.

Non-trading companies are expressly excluded from utilizing the various advantageous provisions of Listings Policy Statement No. 17. This exclusion operates to preclude the Exchange from giving to non-trading companies the special policy relief afforded to inactive trading companies. It also operates to exclude the granting of additional principals' shares to the principals of non-trading companies. The White Paper of the Special Policy Committee and Listings Policy Statement No. 17 state that non-trading companies, in order to have their trading suspension removed, would have to undertake a reorganization which would result in the company meeting the Exchange's minimum initial listing requirements. Although the White Paper indicated that some exceptions to this rule may be allowed if the company meets the minimum listing maintenance requirements, the White Paper noted that, at a minimum, the initial filing should consist of a full business plan. The White Paper also noted that the Exchange will prohibit the issuance of any shares by this type of company until it is in good standing with respect to all filings.

LISTING MAINTENANCE REQUIREMENTS

The Special Policy Committee White Paper noted that the Exchange was the only recognized exchange which did not have listing maintenance requirements, that is, requirements which a listed company had to maintain at all times. That Committee recommended, and the Exchange adopted, requirements involving five separate areas. These requirements are now set out in Listings Policy Statement No. 24 and deal with shareholder distribution, market capitalization, financial condition, financial reporting and the payment of Exchange fees.

With respect to shareholder distribution, a company must have a minimum of 300,000 free-trading shares held by the public (excluding insiders, as that term is defined in s.1(1) of the *Securities Act*, of the company). Within the first year of full listing, a company must have a minimum of 200 public shareholders each holding a board lot or more of free-trading shares. After the first year of listing, a company must have a minimum of 100 public shareholders each holding a board lot or more of free-trading shares.

With respect to market capitalization, the market value of the shares (excluding escrow shares) of a resource company must exceed $150,000.00.

The market value of the shares (excluding escrow shares) of a non-resource company must exceed $200,000.00.

The financial condition requirements are the most complex. A resource company must have net working capital exceeding $25,000.00 or an amount considered adequate to cover six months of general and administrative expenses. In addition, the company's assets must be equal to or greater than 150% of its liabilities (or a solvency ratio of 1:5). A non-resource company must have net working capital exceeding $50,000.00 or an amount considered adequate to cover twelve months of selling, general and administrative expenses. In addition, the company's assets must be equal to or greater than its liabilities (or a solvency ratio of 1).

When calculating net working capital, the Exchange will normally exclude receivables due from, and liabilities payable to, non-arm's length persons and related parties. In addition, where the Exchange deems it appropriate, goodwill and deferred administration expenses may be excluded when calculating a company's total assets unless the company has satisfied the Exchange that such expenses have contributed or are likely to contribute to the future operations of the company. It is recognized by the Exchange that there may be instances where an operating company is not adversely affected if it does not meet the prescribed minimum maintenance financial tests. In such cases, the Exchange may waive the need to comply with one or more of the prescribed minimum requirements if warranted by other financial criteria. A waiver of this type may be subject to review at any time or subject to other conditions which the Exchange may impose. For example, as referred to in Listings Policy Statement No. 17, the Exchange may waive the minimum working capital requirement if the listed company has sufficient income from operations to meet all liabilities as they become due and maintain operations. The asset to liability ratio may be waived if debt service capability is adequate.

With respect to financial reporting, a listed company must be in compliance with the financial reporting requirements of the *Regulation to the Securities Act*. In addition, all financial reports filed with the Securities Commission must be filed with the Exchange.

A listed company must not have any overdue fees payable to the Exchange. This includes annual sustaining fees, filing fees and any other fees which may be specified by the Exchange.

The Exchange may suspend trading in the securities of any listed company which is not in maintenance standing. However, enforcement of the working capital requirement is intended only to be carried out where the company is deficient in one or more of the maintenance requirements in addition to working capital; enforcement of the working capital requirement in and of itself is not intended. Normally, the Exchange will not suspend trading without first giving the listed company notice that it is in default of any of the maintenance requirements and allowing the company a period of ten business days in which to acknowledge or dispute the notice before a trading suspension decision is made by the Exchange. If a trading suspension decision is made, the Exchange will provide a warning notice to the company of the pending suspension and that trading may continue to allow the company a reasonable period of time in which to achieve maintenance standing. As a guideline, ninety days will be the maximum period within which the listed company must satisfy the maintenance requirements from the time is has been declared in default of the maintenance requirements.

As discussed earlier in this Chapter, the maintenance requirements are to be used as the objective or standard to be achieved by companies which have been deemed inactive in order to maintain their listing, even though they may not have completed their reorganization. The maintenance requirements may also be enforced for a company that is below the standards for all or most of the maintenance requirements but may not necessarily fit the definition of an inactive company. The Exchange may require compliance with any aspect of the maintenance requirements following a suspension in trading which resulted from the listed company violating an Exchange policy or rule.

The maintenance requirements are also the standard which is to be reached by companies that have been suspended or cease traded for any reason, for a period of time of less than three months. As a guideline, a company which has been suspended for not more than ten business days, or halted for a reverse take-over pursuant to Listings Policy Statement No. 22 that eventually failed to complete, may be reinstated for trading based on both a plan to achieve maintenance standing and public disclosure of its affairs that are satisfactory to the Exchange.

A company which has had its securities suspended from trading for less than three months must be able to demonstrate to the Exchange that it is in maintenance standing before the Exchange will reinstate trading in its securities. A company which remains suspended for a period of three months or more or becomes subject to Securities Commission Local Policy Statement No. 3-35 (October 13, 1989) may be required to meet the minimum initial listing requirements of the Exchange before trading in the securities of the company is reinstated.

CHAPTER EIGHTEEN

Timely Disclosure

THE RULE

A. General

The legal principle which forms the cornerstone of the securities regulatory framework requires full, true and plain disclosure of all material facts relating to securities where they are being issued in the first instance. In the case of secondary trading, a trade in a previously issued security, the principle of full disclosure takes on a particular meaning. A trade on the Exchange, excepting initial distributions and trades comprising Exchange offerings, is a secondary trade. The applicable rule, called the timely disclosure rule, requires the nature and substance of all material changes in the affairs of a listed company to be promptly disclosed to the investing public by the listed company issuing a news release.

The purpose of such a rule is related to the efficiency of the capital markets. If there is an equality of information upon which to base investment decisions between buyers and sellers, then presumably the chancered price will represent the value of the security being traded. If such is not the case, as where material information is not issued in a timely fashion or is otherwise inaccurate, then the pricing mechanism cannot be expected to operate effectively.

There are however two other opposing interests which come into play when one discusses the timely disclosure rule. First, listed companies must not be too constrained in what they must make public for business reasons. In other words, they must be permitted to exploit business opportunities to the fullest and to carry on their business in such a way as to not be required to disclose all their plans to competitors. Second, the capital markets must be protected from premature disclosure. This is particularly true for the type of speculative securities listed for trading on the Exchange. Premature disclosure will not only adversely affect the public's perception of the integrity of the free market, but will also create destabilizing confusion.

There are three sources for the current timely disclosure rule. There is Listings Policy Statement No. 10, s.67 of the *Securities Act* and the statutory pronouncement takes precedence over the Listings Policy Statement. The third source is National Policy Statement No. 40, first issued by the Superintendent of Brokers in his Notice (March 12, 1987), and which became effective December 1, 1987. This particular Policy Statement, derived from the Toronto Stock Exchange's Policy Statement on timely disclosure, requires the timely disclosure of what is called material information, which is defined as any information relating to the business and affairs of a listed company that results in or would reasonably be expected to result in a significant change in the market price or value of any of the listed company's securities.

B. Material Change

Both Listings Policy Statement No. 10 and s.67 of the *Securities Act* require the prompt public disclosure of a material change. For the purposes of the Exchange rule, a change is material if it might reasonably be expected to affect materially the value of the listed company's securities. For the purposes of the *Act*, a change is defined in s.1(1) to be material if the change involves a change in the company's business, operations, assets or ownership that would reasonably be expected to have a significant effect on the market price or value of any of the company's securities. It also includes a decision made to implement such a change made by the company's directors or senior management if they believe that confirmation by the company's directors is probable. It should be noted that the current Exchange version of the rule, the *Act* and the National Policy Statement all speak to probable price changes. This perspective is preferable to the view expressed in the previous version of Exchange Listings Policy Statement (April 9, 1984) which required disclosure of changes where the reasonable expectation of the effect of the announcement *could* result in a sudden change in price. In this context it should be observed that what may be material facts in a prospectus or an SMF need not necessarily be material for purposes of the timely disclosure rule. For example, a prospectus must disclose all options on a particular company's shares; an option would only be material for the purposes of the timely disclosure rule if its existence can reasonably be expected to cause a significant effect on the market price of the optionor's securities.

It should also be noted that our version of the rule does not go as far as the American version. In *SEC v Texas Gulf Sulphur*, (1968) 401 Federal Reports 2d 833, material was defined to include any information which a reasonable man would attach importance to in determining whether to buy or sell a particular listed security. This test is much broader than the timely disclosure rule discussed above since the former is not limited to the probable effect on the price of the security in question. Furthermore, and this must be stressed, since the timely disclosure rule focuses on price changes, it requires the prompt public disclosure of favourable and unfavourable changes. For example, there is a commonly held view that only favourable drilling results obtained on a resource property must be made the subject of a news release. That view is not correct. Unfavourable drilling results, whether obtained from all drill holes or just some of the holes, must be disclosed in precisely the same way as good results. Similarly, while it is commonly understood that the entering into of a material transaction must be publicly announced, it does not seem to be understood that the disposition of the same asset should be announced. This is particularly true in the case of junior companies because they do not have the large asset base of established enterprises.

Notwithstanding the subjective nature of the material change test, a number of corporate events have, over time, come to be regarded as material changes. A checklist (taken in part from National Policy Statement No. 40) of the more common items, set out in no particular order of importance, is as follows:

- the entering into of any agreement to issue or option a significant amount of securities;
- a change in share or other security ownership which may affect the control of the company;
- any significant change in the senior management or directors of the company;
- proposed changes in the capital structure such as reorganizations, consolidations, subdivisions or amalgamations;
- any change in the undertaking of the company;
- take-over bids or issuer bids;
- borrowing significant funds or hypothecating major assets for loans;
- any non-arm's length transactions;
- the entering or losing of significant contracts; and
- the initiation, discontinuance or other result of significant litigation.

This list does not include occurrences which the Exchange deems to be material and are events for which it requires a listed company to issue a news release. These occurrences include the granting of any incentive stock options, one listed company proposing to acquire shares of another listed company with common insiders, the entering of all private placements, any proposal to issue additional principals' shares and any proposed reverse take-over.

C. Timing of Announcements

As mentioned above, a timely disclosure announcement must be made upon the occurrence of a material change. An error on either side of the right time can have equally adverse consequences for the issuer, its shareholders and the investing public generally. This issue involves two, quite distinct questions. First is that of when an event becomes material; second, assuming an event to be material, when it has to be disclosed.

One of the best ways of resolving these questions is to determine whether the disclosure of a particular event at a given point in time would be more misleading than informative. It seems to be agreed that if an event can be reported as a fact rather than as an opinion or speculation, then it should be made public. For example, if only three out of four required parties to a potential material contract have indicated agreement with its proposed terms, an announcement, even if the listed company is one of the three parties, would be premature. It is only appropriate to announce the entering of the agreement when the fourth party has agreed to all the basic terms of the agreement. (That is not to say that a listed company must wait until the formal agreements have been executed by all parties, although, in some cases, that may be a prudent course of action.) This is appropriate for two reasons. First, the definition of material change in the *Securities Act* specifically contemplates situations where the directors of the listed company have not made a final decision. In these cases, disclosure must be made when the listed company's senior management believe that the directors will probably confirm the decision. Second, disclosure should probably be made when there is basic agreement to all material terms, even though all the details may not have been documented.

What about negotiations? This issue is a significant one in light of the many news releases one sees issued by companies listed on the Exchange. There are a number of comments which may be made on this subject. First, if a listed company has been inactive or dormant, the fact that some negotiations concerning a material contract have started probably represents a material change, particularly in the case of a listed company with no significant assets. In these cases, the public investment information base, in the absence of a news release, would be incomplete. After the issuance of a news release, shareholders of the listed company who sell are probably of the view that the negotiations will not be successful. Investors who buy have the quite opposite viewpoint, and this speculation is legitimate in the circumstances. However, where a listed company is otherwise conducting, and where in the ordinary course of events it would be involved in certain types of negotiations on a more or less routine basis, it is submitted that the announcement of negotiations concerning a potential material asset acquisition is more promotional than informational in nature. In these types of cases, it should be readily apparent that investment decisions turn more in the nature of gambling as opposed to legitimate speculation.

What about intentions? It is not unusual to see news releases announcing a listed company's intention to effect what would otherwise be a material change. The mere intention to implement a material change, unless it is fully within the power of the listed company to do so, would not likely be reportable until a later time, assuming the material change actually occurs.

D. What Must be Disclosed?

The provisions of the *Securities Act* require the disclosure of the nature and the substance of the material change. That is not very informative. The relevant Exchange Listings Policy Statement provides that news releases should contain sufficient details to indicate the nature of the change to enable investors to formulate investment decisions. That Policy Statement also concedes that news releases need not contain all the details concerning the change that would be included in a prospectus or similar document.

In Chapter 9 of the *Exchange Listings Policy and Procedures Manual*, the Exchange deals with an example involving the hypothetical acquisition by a listed company of a mineral property. In commenting on the disclosure requirements, the Exchange indicates that the date of the acquisition agreement should be published, the location and size of the property should be specified, the timing of any proposed exploration on the property should be revealed, the cost to the listed company should be stated and the general character of any proposed exploration programs should be dealt with.

The Exchange's policy requires that news releases be factual and balanced, neither over-emphasizing favourable news nor under-emphasizing unfavourable news. In other words, there must be fair treatment given to the facts being announced. This particular principle should not only be limited in its application to individual news releases, but should also be applied generally. Separate news releases should not describe the same event differently. A release should communicate a change clearly, accurately, and should not contain puffery, exaggeration, or comments designed to colour its interpretation.

A special requirement of the Exchange is that all news releases contain a disclaimer to the effect that the Exchange has not reviewed and does not accept responsibility for either the adequacy or accuracy of a news release. The presence of this disclaimer should not be taken to mean that the Exchange does not review certain news releases nor is the Exchange estopped from taking action against a listed company or its management in cases where it regards a news release to be confusing or otherwise prejudicial to the public interest.

E. How Must Disclosure be Made?

One of the more specific parts of both Listings Policy Statement No. 10 and s.67 of the *Securities Act* deals with the issue of how to make timely disclosure of a material change. Both require the prompt issuance, by the listed company, of a news release.

Prior to April 15, 1988, while the previous Exchange Listings Policy Statement in force (April 9, 1984) required news releases to be issued in a manner which provided for wide dissemination, the actual practice saw a required number of copies of the news release delivered to the Exchange. The Exchange itself would redistribute the releases to its Trading Floor and make them available to the media and widely distributed recognized newsletters.

On April 15, 1988, the provisions of a new, revised Listings Policy Statement, No. 10, came into effect. The substantive change made in the revised Policy Statement was a requirement that the listed company itself had to decide on the manner in which the news had to be disseminated. Moreover, the Exchange adopted a rule which, in the main, requires listed companies to use fee for service news dissemination agencies with nationally integrated disclosure networks to disseminate material change announcements (as opposed to other types of announcements) or else be faced with trading halts pending dissemination of the corporate news. While the latter was unclear when the new Listings Policy was initially announced, it was clarified to a certain extent in a subsequent Exchange Notice (April 28, 1988). Accordingly, when the management of a listed company concludes that a given change is material, they then must choose whether to use a fee for service news dissemination agency. If the latter is not the chosen dissemination mechanism, then the Exchange will halt trading in the company's listed securities until there has been full dissemination. If the management decides that a given change is not material, then it may resort to using dissemination services other than the fee for service news disseminators. It should be noted that, by the express terms of Listings Policy Statement No. 10, the granting of incentive options limited share issuances or acquisitions and changes to the company's roster of directors or officers, need not be considered material for the purpose of the Policy Statement.

The Exchange also requires than an originally signed news release be filed with it, together with three copies thereof, contemporaneously with its issuance by the listed company. The listed company must indicate in a covering letter the manner in which the news release was disseminated. If it is impractical for one of the company's directors or appropriate officer to sign the news release, then it may be signed on their behalf by an authorized agent. When it is not possible to file the originally signed news release on its issuance, then the Exchange will accept a facsimile or telex copy as long as an originally signed copy is filed with the Exchange within five days of the date of the telex news release.

A copy of the news release must be filed as soon as practicable after its issuance with the Securities Commission. In addition, a material change report form (*Securities Act*, Form 27) must be filed with the Securities Commission as soon as possible and, in any event, within ten days after the date on which the change occurs. That form requires the listed company to indicate the date of the material change, the date and places of issuance of the news release as well as a summary, and a full description, of the material change in question. The company must also give the name and business telephone number of a senior officer who is knowledgeable about both the material change and the material change report form. This latter requirement is to enable the Securities Commission's staff to contact the listed company should it desire to do so.

F. Confidential Material Change

As pointed out above, one of the *bona fide* competing principles to the requirement to publicly announce all material changes is the principle that such disclosure should not operate so as to require the listed company's directors to act detrimentally to the interests of the company in breach of their fiduciary duties as directors. Accordingly, both the Exchange and the *Securities Act* recognize that there are situations where prompt disclosure may be deferred until a later time. The Exchange permits non-public disclosure when to do so is essential to the welfare of the listed company. The provisions of s.67(2) of the *Act* permit such non-disclosure where to do otherwise would be unduly detrimental to the interests of the listed company. As should be apparent, this does not mean that unfavourable news can be withheld. Rather, it means that the disclosure would be harmful to the listed company in that this disclosure would conflict with the fiduciary duties of the directors to act in the best interests of the listed company. For example, if a listed company makes a significant discovery on its resource property, it may delay announcing the discovery until it has had enough time to stake or otherwise acquire adjacent claims. In this situation, the listed company is required to advise the Exchange of the situation so that it can monitor trading in the company's shares for a trading pattern which indicates that confidentiality has not been maintained.

In addition to advising the Exchange, the listed company must immediately file, on a confidential basis, a Form 27 with the Securities Commission. In that form, the company must disclose the change in sufficient detail to permit the Securities Commission staff to determine whether it wishes to avoid disclosure of the information on the basis that this outweighs the adherence to the principle of public disclosure. The Securities Commission must be updated on a ten day basis as to the need or desirability to continue to keep the information confidential.

During the time when a material change is kept confidential, all persons associated with the listed company who have knowledge of that information must refrain from trading in the securities of the listed company. The *Act*, in s.68, specifically prohibits persons who have a special relationship with the listed company from trading in the period of time during which the change is kept confidential. This is what is called a modified tipper-tippee rule. A person is in a special relationship to a listed company if the person is a director, officer or employee of the listed company or its subsidiary, is an insider of the listed company or its subsidiary, is a professional adviser to the company who has acquired knowledge of the information, or is a person who has acquired knowledge of the confidential information from one of the foregoing persons and knew or ought reasonably to have known that this person fell into one or more of the foregoing class of persons.

PRECIOUS METALS ASSAYS

In the early Spring of 1988, the Exchange became concerned about a growing tendency on the part of some listed companies to use non-fire assay methods to analyze the precious metal contents of samples taken from their properties. While the express concern related to the use of unknown, mostly foreign, laboratories, and the utilizing of unqualified personnel, the main concern was directed at listed companies using secret, or proprietary, techniques and unverified techniques as the basis for public announcements. As a result of these concerns, on March 18, 1988, in a letter written to securities lawyers and all listed companies, the Exchange announced that each news release, shareholder report or other public communication which included precious metal test results by non-Canadian laboratories, utilizing any technique other than the fire assay method, must contain certain specific information, namely: the analytical method employed, the name of the laboratory where the samples were analyzed, and the results of any fire assay check program. If a fire assay check program was not undertaken, then the listed company's intention to do so at an independent laboratory must be specified. The results must be published in what the Exchange considers to be a timely manner. A failure on the part of a listed company to comply with this Exchange directive may have trading in its listed securities halted pending compliance with the policy.

CHAPTER NINETEEN

Trading and Delisting Matters

TRADING DELAY

The Exchange is permitted, under Exchange Rule C.1.03.2 to delay trading briefly in the securities of a listed company until a time which is not later than the end of the current trading session. Except in rare circumstances, trading delays usually do not exceed one hour in duration.

Trading delays may be instituted by the Exchange in one of two circumstances. The first is where an imbalance of orders in a particular listed company's shares has developed. In this situation which creates either the potential for, or an actual, rapid price increase or decrease, the Exchange uses the delay to give the floor traders, as well as their brokers and clients, an opportunity to reassess the market. If the imbalance continues, and the Trading Floor Manager will be able to determine this quite expeditiously, the delay will be continued to give the Exchange the opportunity to set up and operate a book on the trading floor through which the imbalance in orders may be rectified.

A trading delay also occurs where there are unexplained changes in the price of the listed company's securities.

It should be noted that there is no permanent record maintained by the Exchange describing trading delays. With all other types of trading stoppages, the Exchange issues Exchange Notices, which appear in the Exchange's Daily Bulletin; a copy of this Notice is filed as part of the public record associated with each listed company.

TRADING HALT

The most common type of Exchange trading stoppage is the halt trading order. Under the provisions of Exchange Rule C.1.03, a trading halt order may be imposed against the listed securities of a particular company for any one of three reasons. A trading halt may be ordered where a listed company has breached any of the terms of its listing agreement and has not remedied the breach. A halt may be ordered where a material change in the affairs of a listed company may have occurred but has not been publicly announced by way of the issuance of a news release by that listed company. A halt trading order is ordered when, in the opinion of the Exchange, a circumstance exists which could materially affect the public interest. This catch-all provision is designed to give the Exchange absolute authority over the trading of a listed company's shares through its facilities.

Unlike a trading delay, a trading halt, while sometimes routine in character, represents a serious incursion into the listed company's privilege to have its shares traded on a continuous basis. Accordingly, as a matter of practice, it is ordered only by senior Exchange officials.

It must be recognized that a halt trading order extends only to trading on the Trading Floor of the Exchange; it does not otherwise operate to prevent treasury issuances by the listed company nor does it prevent secondary trading other than through the facilities of the Exchange.

The most common reason for the instituting of a trading halt by the Exchange occurs where there has been a material change in the business or affairs of a listed company and no public disclosure of the particulars of that material change has been made by the company in accordance with the Exchange's timely disclosure rule. If the listed company does not request, on its own motion, a trading halt, then the Exchange itself will order a trading halt which will last until such time as the details of the material change have been announced and disseminated to the satisfaction of the Exchange. In most cases, the detection of these situations is initially made by the Exchange's market surveillance section, using the Electronic Market Monitoring System, because of a significant movement in the trading price or volume of the listed company's stock. Where, in fact, a material change has not occurred, the Exchange will often issue a halt trading order nonetheless, pending the publication and dissemination of what are called no material change news releases. These releases indicate that no material change has occurred and that management has no knowledge of any facts upon which the price movement can be based.

More often than not, however, a material change has occurred and has not, for one reason or another, been announced by the listed company. In these circumstances, the Exchange will routinely indicate that a trading halt is in order and give the listed company the opportunity to request a halt. In these situations, the position of the Exchange is an ultimatum: either the listed company will request the halt or the Exchange will, as it is empowered to do, make the order itself. In cases where the company itself has requested the order, whether voluntarily or at the urging of the Exchange, the Exchange Notice will indicate that the halt was at the request of the listed company. In all other cases, the Exchange Notice will indicate that the halt trading order was issued by the Exchange itself. These latter cases are generally regarded by the investment community to be more serious situations than the former and therefore, in routine situations, the listed company should initiate the halt trading order process.

The Exchange may use a trading halt to enforce its filing requirements. For example, if a Filing Statement has not been filed in a timely manner, the Exchange may, in exceptional circumstances, halt trading until the Filing Statement and other requisite documentation is filed.

Under the subject Rule a trading halt may be maintained until the circumstances giving rise to the halt have been settled to the satisfaction of the Exchange. This does not mean that every trading halt is rescinded, as some are turned into trading suspension orders. However, most are rescinded a short time after they are instituted. When they are rescinded, an Exchange Notice disclosing that fact is issued. The Notice also contains the trading day on, and time at, which trading is to be resumed.

TRADING SUSPENSION

Under the provisions of Exchange Rule C.1.05, the Exchange, through its President or any Vice-President, may suspend trading on the Trading Floor in a listed company's securities where any of the circumstances set out in Exchange Rule C.1.03 exist or where it otherwise considers it to be in the public interest to do so. The effect of a trading suspension order takes the securities out of the posted and called for trading category, thus the carrying value for margin brokerage purposes must be fixed at zero. In the case of a halt trading order, which only affects the callability of the affected securities (they remain listed and posted for trading), there is no adverse impact on the carrying value of the particular securities. Thus, a trading suspension order is regarded by the investment community as a serious signal being sent by the Exchange.

For the most part, the reasons forming the basis for a halt trading order will form the initial basis of a trading suspension where the circumstances which gave rise to the trading halt are not resolved to the satisfaction of the Exchange within a reasonable period of time. Only rarely will a trading suspension order be issued in the first instance. It will, however, be used where the infraction is a serious or flagrant one such as where a listed company refuses to follow a request or an order repeatedly made to it by the Exchange.

There are two special situations where a trading suspension will automatically be issued by the Exchange. First, trading will be suspended for one complete trading session in situations where the Exchange concludes that a listed company has intentionally breached an important Exchange requirement. In this situation, an Exchange Notice describing the non-compliance and duration of the suspension will be issued. The second special situation is in cases when the Securities Commission, or the Superintendent of Brokers, has issued a cease trading order under s.144 of the *Securities Act* against the securities of a listed company. In this case, an Exchange Notice will be issued describing the reasons for, and terms of, the cease trading order.

TRADING CANCELLATION

Under the provisions of Exchange Rule C.1.24, the Exchange is empowered to disallow any trade made through its facilities which is deemed unreasonable. This power, under the Rule, may only be exercised during or at the close of the trading session during which the trade was made. Under the Rule, the power may be exercised only by the Trading Floor Manager. The Rule is silent on exactly what has to be unreasonable, however, it is interpreted by the Exchange as relating only to the price per share of a particular trade and then, only in relation to a subsequent price. Because of its judgmental character, this particular provision is rarely utilized by the Exchange.

Under the provisions of Exchange Rule C.2.35, an almost identical power is provided and is not as circumscribed as the Rule described above. Under Rule C.2.35, a power is given to the Exchange to cancel or alter any trade without there being any specific prerequisite condition to enable the power to be used. The power appears to be unfettered. That interpretation is probably not correct and the better view is that the Rule is circumscribed by elements associated with prejudice to the interest of the investing public generally. The Rule has been used most often to cancel trades made by an insider in cases where the Exchange has concluded that the insider has made use of knowledge of material facts or material changes in trading the securities of the relevant listed company. This Rule has also been used to cancel trades made on inaccurate information which had been widely disseminated.

DELISTING

Under the provisions of Exchange Rule B.2.01, the Exchange is empowered to delist the listed securities of any listed company. This is to be distinguished from the circumstance where the listed company itself requests a delisting, which of course is a voluntary delisting. The delisting forming the topic of Rule B.2.00 is involuntary in nature, and one which is generally opposed by both the management of the listed company and its shareholders.

The umbrella, or catch-all, delisting power is contained in Exchange Rule B.2.01 which provides that the Exchange may use the delisting power in cases where a listed company ceases to meet any of the minimum listing requirements which may apply to it or if the Exchange is otherwise of the opinion that it would be in the public interest to do so. The strict application of this Rule would lead to a substantial number of delistings. Accordingly, the power is used selectively and judiciously, and only in cases where there are significant non-compliance problems which have not been remedied over a reasonable length of time, to the satisfaction of the Exchange. At this juncture, two things should be mentioned. Delisting is usually fatal to a company, unless it is listed quickly elsewhere, because there is no over-the-counter market in British Columbia. Different considerations apply to the delisting of a company's securities than originally apply to its initial listing since its shareholders now comprise the investing public. That is, the insiders of the company have been permitted to resell their securities of the company to the investing public. Accordingly, the Exchange cannot capriciously delist companies. Rather, delisting is the final solution to an unresolved problem. It is for this reason that listed companies will, and should, be given a reasonable opportunity to correct deficiencies insofar as maintaining minimum listing standards are concerned.

Exchange Rule B.2.02 sets out five specific circumstances in which the Exchange may issue a delisting order, the first of which occurs where the financial condition of the listed company is unsatisfactory and does not warrant a continuation of a listing. Companies put into receivership for winding up, or which file for, or are petitioned into, bankruptcy would fall into this category. A test for financial condition which the Exchange seems to use on an annual basis is the test of whether a listed company pays its annual sustaining fee. If, despite numerous reminders, the annual sustaining fee for a specific company is not paid, the Exchange will delist its securities. When the listed company fails to maintain the prescribed minimum number of public shareholders to the point where public trading in the company's securities is inappropriate, the Exchange may issue a delisting order. However, this is one situation which may be remedied relatively easily by the company in question conducting an Exchange offering. Usually, the Exchange gives the company the opportunity to arrange such a financing. In some cases, such as following a successful take-over bid, the design may have been to render the company, in essence, a private company. These situations usually involve voluntary delistings however, on occasion, the Exchange has had to resort to this head of delisting to prevent what is otherwise a private company from remaining listed on the Exchange.

The Exchange may issue a delisting order where a listed company has become a shell company (one which has no operating assets or has discontinued its operations or business). This type of example has, in the past, rarely resulted in the Exchange issuing an order to delist the company's listed securities. However, given the Exchange's new maintenance listing standards, it can be expected that orders under this Rule will increase as the Exchange deals with inactive listed companies.

A delisting order also occurs where the listed company has failed to comply with the listing agreement in a material respect or has otherwise failed to comply with applicable Exchange requirements. The last circumstance in which the Exchange will issue a delisting order involves a listed company failing to comply with the Exchange's timely disclosure rule. It was thought that the importance of this particular policy should be stressed, and so it was added as the fifth basis for involuntary delistings. Once again, unless the situation is irreversible, the Exchange usually gives the company concerned an opportunity to rectify the problem before delisting becomes an issue.

The Exchange, in addition to having Exchange Rule B.2.00 covering delistings, has recently adopted Listings Policy Statement No. 25. This Policy Statement is mainly complementary to Exchange Rule B.2.00 insofar as involuntary delistings are concerned as it does not contain any circumstance for delisting not already enumerated by that Rule. It does, however, provide that in some cases the circumstances giving rise to the delisting potential may be out of the company's control. A failure to maintain the prescribed minimum public distribution requirements after the completion of a take-over bid may represent an example of such a circumstance. So long as the company continues to have a project of merit, the Exchange may defer the issuing of a delisting order if it is satisfied that the particular problem can be resolved within a reasonable time period.

The Policy Statement does contain new principles with respect to voluntary delisting. In this regard, the Policy Statement provides that if there is an alternative market for the company's securities, such as a recognized stock exchange or a NASDAQ quotation, then the Exchange will facilitate a delisting request. Where, however, there is no such market, the Exchange primarily will be concerned to ensure that the company's public shareholders, and the investing public generally, will not be prejudiced by the delisting. Where the Exchange decides that it should issue a delisting order, the company will be required to issue a news release disclosing its plans. The Exchange, under these circumstances, may delay the delisting to facilitate the orderly settlement of trades and to allow shareholders to sell to willing purchasers. In most cases, an Exchange Notice will be issued 10 days prior to the delisting.

Index

181